Also by JOHN O'MEARA

THE MODERN DEBACLE
and *OUR HOPE IN THE GODDESS*

SHAKESPEARE, THE GODDESS,
and *MODERNITY*

MYTH, DEPRAVITY, IMPASSE

◆

Graves, Shakespeare, Keats

John O'Meara

iUniverse, Inc.
Bloomington

MYTH, DEPRAVITY, IMPASSE
Graves, Shakespeare, Keats

Copyright © 2008, 2011 John O'Meara

All rights reserved. No part of this book may be used or reproduced by any means, graphic, electronic, or mechanical, including photocopying, recording, taping or by any information storage retrieval system without the written permission of the publisher except in the case of brief quotations embodied in critical articles and reviews.

iUniverse books may be ordered through booksellers or by contacting:

iUniverse
1663 Liberty Drive
Bloomington, IN 47403
www.iuniverse.com
1-800-Authors (1-800-288-4677)

Because of the dynamic nature of the Internet, any Web addresses or links contained in this book may have changed since publication and may no longer be valid. The views expressed in this work are solely those of the author and do not necessarily reflect the views of the publisher, and the publisher hereby disclaims any responsibility for them.

Any people depicted in stock imagery provided by Thinkstock are models, and such images are being used for illustrative purposes only.

Certain stock imagery © Thinkstock.

ISBN: 978-0-595-47643-5 (sc)
ISBN: 978-0-595-91907-9 (e)

Printed in the United States of America

iUniverse rev. date: 11/15/2011

Contents

Preface ix

The Mythic Ground 1

The Worst of Depravity 33

Impasse of the Imagination 55

Endnotes 73

once again
for

*A*LINE

Preface

This book is a kind of compendium of thought about the mythical and what it represents as an idea of experience. Hence, my review of the various positions taken about myth by some of the more prominent modern theorists of myth, which I offer as a background to Graves in the book's first chapter. The questions I start from are the following: What are we to make of the astounding fact that Graves would appear to have successfully penetrated again into an objective mythical experience? And how far are we from any such prospect ourselves? To conceive of the Goddess appearing to us again with an actual pictoriality that arises out of the mythical world she inhabits, quite objectively, makes us profoundly uneasy and puts us in mind of how alien we are to such a projected experience. Graves blamed a long history of unreal rationalism for that sense of alienation, and Ted Hughes followed suit with an application of the same moral, basing himself on his own exhaustive study of Shakespeare's relationship to the Goddess in *Shakespeare and the Goddess of Complete Being*.

In this book I argue from the assumption that an objective mythical experience *should be* possible for us today, following the lead of Graves, but I proceed speculatively, accommodating our profound uneasiness about such an experience. However, I do not let the modern sceptic off easily. There is more than simply "a willing suspension of disbelief" in the approach I take to the idea of such an experience. In fact, I *commit* to it, taking exception to the easy conclusions of modern scepticism on the one side and the overly confident spirit of Hughes and of Graves on the other. Shakespeare's work I focus on as another way of assessing what it means for us to engage in a mythical experience today. For from Shakespeare we learn that there is far more to contend with in our inner make-up than what Graves or Hughes maintain, and that more will, therefore, have to be known about that make-up, before we can permit ourselves the kind of full engagement with our natures that the mythical experience requires of us.

The idea of such an experience remains, for all the commitment that is registered about it in one form or another, profoundly uncertain, and I also bring Keats in to show how our modern scepticism emerges in relation to it. However, I am just as bent on showing that, in our appreciation of Keats, we have thought *ourselves* into his position more than we are justified in doing. For Keats would appear to be no less committed to the idea of recovering mythical experience than are Graves and Shakespeare, and this in spite of his pronounced modern tendencies, which become for him, as I show, at a certain point a trap.

In my chapter on Graves, I stop to consider the views of Eliade, Cassirer, Jung, Barfield and Campbell. Thereafter, I build on a more modest range of primarily literary views of Shakespeare and of Keats, to suit my own emphasis. A special place is allotted in my presentation to the views on *Macbeth* as provided by James Calderwood and Harry Berger Jr. and to the views on Keats of W. Jackson Bate and John Middleton Murry. Far from being a comprehensive treatment, my chapters on those authors gradually slip away into a more direct presentation of my themes, as these seem to me to be illuminated by the literature itself. The effect, towards the end, will thus appear fragmentary, but that will seem appropriate to a book that reflects on our fundamental uncertainty in relation to the three questions that are raised:

- *Where do we stand in relation to the objective ground of myth?*
- *Where do we stand in relation to the depravity in our nature?*
- *What* **do** *we make of ourselves in supposing ourselves defined by a use of the Imagination developed in relation to ourselves alone?*

All three questions are brought forward here, what's more, inasmuch as three male poets, writing out of a basically male perspective, reflect to us our sense of what can come of these questions. I have attempted to bring these diverse matters together not with any notion that they have fully clarified in relation to each other—there would still be a need for the additional input that a woman's perspective would have to offer on these questions[1]; I bring these matters together here out of the view that for now they summarize *among themselves* the issue of what our relationship to mythical experience can be about. The common link among these three areas of focus is to a mythical unity that all three authors I treat of acknowledge as the ultimate goal of our experience. However, each of these authors assumes a relationship to this unity that is at once concrete and abstract, the element of abstraction in each author's relationship to unity being the measure of the unrealized portion of his involvement in it. We can only hope, therefore, that along will come another, a fourth, who will have the fuller resources needed, and the right audience, to begin to show us how, working out of all three areas, we can indeed make our way back to the mythical unity in which all will be resolved.

I
THE MYTHIC GROUND

I

In a public lecture[2] given at the Y.M.H.A. Centre in New York in 1957, Robert Graves directly addressed the ground of his mythical faith with the potentially explosive question:

> *Do I think that poets are literally inspired by the White Goddess?*

From the context of his address it is clear that Graves was not led to this question himself. It is prefaced by a remark that indicates it is being aired in response to signs of disbelief in his audience that he could be taking his claims so far. Graves's response to his question is a carefully crafted piece of evasive affirmation:

> *Some of you are looking queerly at me. Do I think that poets are literally inspired by the White Goddess? That is an improper question. What would you think, should I ask you if, in your opinion, the Hebrew prophets were literally inspired by God? Whether God is a metaphor or a fact cannot be reasonably argued; let us likewise be discreet on the subject of the Goddess.*

Rarely was Graves so circumspect in his proclamation of his great Theme. His confidence on this occasion is, in a somewhat unusual way, tempered by the doubt he is addressing in his immediate audience. His subdued tone reflects also the bafflement he appears to have felt about a critique that had been made of his presentation of the White Goddess, in a recent review by Randall Jarrell, the American poet.[3] Jarrell had argued that Graves's picture of the White Goddess was merely a projection of his own personal fantasy. Thus both Jarrell and Graves's audience combine to confront him with an image of the opposition he might expect to find to the *kind* of claims he was making, with their unquestioned assumption about the literal existence, in some sense, of the White Goddess. In the face of this opposition Graves momentarily dampens his claims in respect to how far they might be taken.

I linger over this episode because it points the issue of what someone who claims to have found a literal connection with the mythical will face in his sceptical and uncomprehending audience. With that is raised the whole question of what the ground of a mythical faith can be. One may

4   MYTH, DEPRAVITY, IMPASSE

claim of Graves's lecture as a whole, in comparison with his many other pronouncements, a kind of retreat in the face of the enemy's display of its forces. Thus, for the most part here, he is content to reiterate that aspect of his Theme that is primarily historical. That approach is emphasized by way of making the point that

> *Mr. Jarrell cannot accuse me of **inventing** the White Goddess…*

Hence, also, his further statement that

> *It is enough for me to quote the myths and give them historical sense…*

And it is with this less-than-muted sense of being in the presence of the enemy that Graves proffers what is for him the comparatively reduced declaration, intended to set him on safe ground, that

> *I hold that critical notice should be taken of the Goddess.*

"Notice" of this kind is due because of the coherent "grammar of poetic myth" that Graves was known to have derived from his historical studies of the Goddess cult. Even Jarrell acknowledges that he is grateful for it, for on the basis of this "grammar" Graves was able to write poems that Jarrell describes as "some of the most beautiful poems of our time."[4] Especially is it a matter for Graves of taking notice of the "poetry which deeply affects readers", and how it comes to be. The answer is in "the persistent survival", among the "Muse-poets", of "faith" in the White Goddess—which may be conscious or unconscious. Their "imagery" can be proven to be "drawn" directly from Her cult, and the "magic" of their poems shown to be dependent on "its closeness to her mysteries."

Graves's account, bold as it is, still begs the question of what the ground of this "faith" might be, but, in this lecture at least, he is as sly as his enemy is unyielding. Primarily, he *reverts* (from the claim of literalness) to the view that

> *In scientific terms, no god at all can be proved to exist, but only beliefs in gods, and the effects of such beliefs on worshippers.*

Such a view, Graves maintains, applies as much to the Christian belief

The Mythic Ground   5

in a Father God as to the Jewish belief in the God of the prophets, and, therefore, can apply as much to a belief in the Goddess, whose religion can be attested to on the same grounds. Graves is as uncompromising about his own historical emphasis:

> *The most important single fact in the early history of Western religion and sociology was undoubtedly the gradual suppression of the Lunar Mother-goddess's inspiratory cult, and its supercession by…the busy, rational cult of the Solar God Apollo.*

Of the Goddess's presence in the religion of former times, and of its stubborn survival against the odds into modern times, there can be no doubt, and since poetic inspiration remains, in scientific terms, an undisclosed mystery:

> *…why not attribute inspiration to the Lunar Muse, the oldest and most convenient European term for the source in question?*

It is a triumphant gambit, because of the appeal, in "the *oldest*… European term", to priority in this case. However, Graves goes farther: he implies that, as "Protestant Doctors of Divinity…posit the literal existence of an all-powerful God"—claiming for themselves proofs of "supernatural happenings" in spite of these being "ill-attested" by science—adherents of the Goddess might do the same. There is also the argument from precedent and tradition (a very long tradition in this case), in which Graves deliberately milks the present perfect tense: "In fact, the Goddess has always been…The Muse-poets have always recognized" etc. And it is only *after* Graves has pursued this whole elaborate strategic disarming of the enemy, that we find him shifting back to a claim about the Goddess's literal role in the lives of poets:

> *By ancient religious theory the White Goddess becomes incarnate in her human representative—a priestess, a prophetess, a queen-mother. No Muse-poet can grow conscious of the Muse except by experience of some woman in whom the Muse-power is to some degree or other resident.*

[margin note: An Anima figure]

From a claim from "ancient religious theory", Graves shifts here to a present actuality—"No Muse-poet *can*"—and this shift is now sustained. Finally,

6 MYTH, DEPRAVITY, IMPASSE

we hear from him again in the forthright mode in which his auditors had been accustomed to hearing from him before he came face to face with the opposition his claims provoked:

> *But the real, perpetually obsessed Muse-poet makes a distinction between the Goddess as revealed in the supreme power, glory, wisdom and love of woman, and the individual woman in whom the Goddess may take up residence for a month, a year, seven years, or even longer. The Goddess abides; and it may be that he will again have knowledge of her through his experience of another woman…*

Graves's case is among the most extraordinary instances in modern times of a claim to literalness in the experience of myth, and it is for this reason that I choose to focus on him here. His case is the more extraordinary just because—in his comportment and in his whole manner of expressing himself—he is in every other respect the model of level-headedness, and is so to a fault (which has made him an easy object of caricature). I have also *begun* with the episode of the lecture because *it* represents, on the other side of the issue, a somewhat extreme instance of disobligingness when it comes to responding to a claim of literalness. Between these two extremes the issue of the *ground* of myth is thus raised. The encounter between the two here is not exactly what one would call fruitful; the issue degenerates into polemics, the appeal to "faith" appearing as the appeasing counter to be mutually appropriated by both sides. Perhaps in the case of Graves's audience nothing short of the grossest scientific "proof" would have satisfied the sense of "reality" that needed to be appeased, where only a more subtle order of metaphysical proof could be provided.

The same could hardly be said of Jarrell, however, who is ready in his critique to credit Graves with "poems that almost deserve the literal *magical*"[5]. Only, Jarrell does not intend by "magical" the literal sense that Graves does, where for instance *he* writes, at the beginning of *The White Goddess*, "European poetic lore…is ultimately based on magical principles."[6] In his way of offering praise of Graves's poems—"*almost*…the *literal* magical"—Jarrell mischievously approaches Graves's sense while clearly intending another, very much more restricted one. Jarrell's use of "magical" intensifies the issue in yet another way, inasmuch as our use of the term allows us to draw on a literal connotation of the word where we do not in fact intend one—which we would scrupulously deny if ever held to account for it. Certainly we do not normally intend by it the literal rendering that Graves continues to proclaim, e.g., in his new Foreword to *The White Goddess*, written a few years after the critique by Jarrell:

> *My thesis is that the language of myth anciently current in the Mediterranean and Northern Europe was a magical language bound up with popular religious ceremonies in honour of the Moon-Goddess, or Muse…and that this* **remains** *the language of true poetry…*

And *because* it remains so, Graves was concerned that "poetry of a magical quality" should not continue merely as an incidental or haphazard achievement, the result of "an inspired, almost pathological, reversion to the original language", but should rather be strenuously researched and cultivated, on the clear basis of "a conscientious study of its grammar and vocabulary".

◆   ◆   ◆

But it may be well to continue by looking at the poems by Graves that Jarrell himself describes as "magical"—what he calls the "mythical-archaic poems", among which are two of the best known, "The White Goddess" and "To Juan at the Winter Solstice". Thus we shall put off saying, for the moment, in what a mythical "faith" may be said to consist, or on what "ground" it may be said to be predicated, to consider first what *kind* of world it could be said to proclaim, or what world-view Graves can be said to have committed to on the basis of his experience of the ancient mythical material. We shall, in doing so, also be giving ourselves a chance to see precisely what kind of grammar and vocabulary we can expect to be dealing with.

Much of what Graves understood as to how the Goddess figures in our lives can be said to be contained in these two poems, which we may see as two parts of one whole, with "The White Goddess" (though second in composition) playing the first part to "To Juan". It is the forthrightness of his claims that impress themselves upon us in "The White Goddess". This forthrightness belies the strenuous effort that has been made first to disassociate from the main Western cultural attitudes that have obstructed a proper approach to the Goddess. These are gone into at great length in Graves's book, *The White Goddess*, but they may be summarized here as the 'ascetic' attitude associated with Christianity as well as Western Apollonian rational philosophy. The Goddess, among other things, demands one's engagement *with* the world; it could never be with Her a case of turning away from what the world has fully to offer, also to one's bodily experience and, from within that experience, to one's consciousness.

At the same time, the "journey" that the poem's speaker narrates, into "distant regions" in order to "find" Her, is less a journey across the world than it is a journey *into* Nature[7]:

> *Seeking her out at the volcano's head,*
> *Among pack ice, or where the track had faded*
> *Beyond the cavern of the seven sleepers:*

It is at this point, significantly, that the Goddess Herself arises:

> *Whose broad high brow was white as any leper's,*
> *Whose eyes were blue, with rowan-berried lips,*
> *With hair curled honey-coloured to white hips.*

The idea proposed as to how the Goddess is to be "found" has less to do with the typical mythical journey of the past than with a way of living into Nature that has much in common with latter-day Romantic experience. Thus Jarrell's term, "archaic", does not fit altogether. One need not go far either across the world or back into time to be able, in Graves's view, to "celebrate" the Goddess's presence; one need only be able to live one's "way" fully into Spring, as well as into all of the rest of the natural year.

Here is where the peculiar attitude involved in making the right approach to the Goddess makes itself felt. It must be, if one is to find Her, a matter of living fully into the *whole cycle* of the year, and so *quite as much* into Fall and Winter as into Spring and Summer. That thought defies one's imagination, as much as does the thought that one is to find Her "at the volcano's head" or "Among pack ice", or that, in aspiring to know Her *through* this kind of engagement, one risks, by one's unworthiness, being mentally struck down as by lightning ("the next bright bolt"). Graves reserves the certainty of being so much in tune with the essential Goddess Who lies behind Her natural manifestations—blessed, as he is, "with so huge a sense/Of her *nakedly* worn magnificence"—the possibility of being favored and supported in this venture seems within reach.

In "Juan" an extreme engagement with Nature constitutes again a first point of entry into the Goddess's world:

> *Is it of trees you tell, their months and virtues,*
> *Or strange beasts that beset you,*

> *Of birds that croak at you the Triple will?*

But with "Triple will" we are already into the stuff of myth and very soon, with the further shift to the Zodiac, are suddenly plummeted into an Underworld-drama in which many of the elements of an assumed "faith" are being marshalled:

> *Or of the Zodiac and how slow it turns*
> *Below the Boreal crown,*
> *Prison of all true kings that ever reigned?*

We are asked to think that the Zodiac, as we know it in the outer world, continues in its existence and in its influence *in* this Underworld (though reduced to a slow turning there). This Underworld is also now seen as the

> *Prison of all true kings that ever reigned...*

And before we have had time to consider where we are with these references, we are precipitated through a tremendous drama in which we are asked to see a set of such "victims" given over to a destiny that involves repeated death and re-birth or re-incarnation:

> *Water to water, ark again to ark,*
> *From woman back to woman:*
> *So each new victim treads unfalteringly*
> *The never altered circuit of his fate,*
> *Bringing twelve peers as witness*
> *Both to his starry rise and starry fall.*

It might be thought that by "victims" Graves means every man and that men give *themselves*, like these "true kings", to the same destiny. *They* are "true" because given over to this destiny without reserve. *How* they are brought into the drama is then dramatized, the Goddess Herself appearing here as the main Agent in the "one story and one story only" that is "worth telling":

> *She in her left hand bears a leafy quince;*
> *When with her right she crooks a finger, smiling,*
> *How may the King hold back?*
> *Royally then he barters life for love.*

Summoned, as it were, to death by the Goddess—who assumes here a remarkable doubleness of form—this "King" now submits to what has all the marks of an ancient mythical Underworld-initiation:

> *Or of the undying snake from chaos hatched,*
> *Whose coils contain the ocean,*
> *Into whose chops with naked sword he springs,*
> *Then in black water, tangled by the reeds,*
> *Battles three days and nights,*
> *To be spewed up beside her scalloped shore...*

In the past this initiation was enacted *in some sense* literally[8]. Such initiation involved a microcosmic condensation of the whole experience of the cycle of death and re-birth, which was somehow lived out directly over the course of the "three days and nights" mentioned. The lines in their own terms are a tremendous evocation of the event described. Then Graves comes back, suddenly, to the *present* reality and the "fear" that he knows must lie in his own son's heart from having to submit to this forbidding destiny:

> *Much snow is falling, winds roar hollowly,*
> *The owl hoots from the elder,*
> *Fear in your heart cries to the loving-cup...*

"Fear" is to be countered by trust, in the dependability of the Goddess's "love"; this "love", from Her side, She bestows for the "life" given over to Her. In the meantime the sudden shift back to the present has the effect of emphasizing a man's individual-psychological "distance", in his own life, from the great realities of death and re-birth that have been "mythically" rendered and conceived.

A *literal* continuity between the two spheres is, nevertheless, assumed, and the medial ground is, once again, Nature. The "fear" Graves addresses in his son, and through him in every man, is the fear that haunts him from knowing that he must *go* to his death. Nature in its foreboding and destructive aspect speaks ultimately of the death he must endure. But the hope lies in the "love" that is tendered *out* of this prospect, which *returns* him from that great "ocean" or "sea" of death into which he plunges. He returns because he is *in* the Goddess, Who reserves to Herself the *power* to return, from the great "grapple" with death. And so She is presented at the end of the poem:

Her brow was creamy as the crested wave,
Her sea-grey eyes were wild,
*But nothing promised that is not performed.*⁹

◆   ◆   ◆

The cosmology in which Graves asks us to "believe" is especially marked by this emphasis on a literal connection, through Nature, to the great "sea" of death that the Underworld represents. In its darker, material aspect, Nature is seen as *continuous with* this Underworld. In "The Sea Horse" Graves directly applies himself in his consciousness of this cosmology. Things are still possible, the Goddess's order still accessible, if here only through the dark element that binds the poet to his beloved in an "unquiet love", the mark of their involvement in what makes Her Creation difficult. It is difficult because they share, through their physical nature, in the turmoil projected from the Underworld (from that same "ocean" or "sea" of death as presented in "To Juan"). This turmoil involves them problematically in "pain" along with the "love". The "pain" is connected also with their sexual nature, their sexual needs, which are not to be shied away from. "Renewal" or re-birth comes from the engagement with these needs. From the "blood-red" wound of the sexual encounter comes the "pain" of submission to the physical, which will always be a part of it, but through which "love" is affirmed.

Submission to the dark, material side of the Goddess's Creation *as mythically rendered* is the aspect of Graves's presentation that has met with the most extreme resistance. Resistance has come because of the literal emphasis Graves gives to this rendering. This reaction is especially strong in relation to his portrayal of the White Goddess or Mother of All-Living as "the ancient power of fright and lust—the female spider, the queen bee whose embrace is death."¹⁰ She appears in this guise in the poem "She Is No Liar", where She is imagined "wiping away"

Honey from her lips, blood from her shadowy hand.

Graves's picture of the Goddess is of One Who *generally* submits her devotee to violent dispossession, but in "Lion Lover" Graves depicts himself as one who is only ready to accept his "doom":

Though by the Moon possessed
I gnaw at dry bones in a lost lair

Graves knows himself to be caught up in his physical nature and its confounding deprivation bearing on death. Yet in his submission to this doom he will often be re-paid, the sight of Her "love" appearing to him as a result of his strenuous refusal of any other more appealing life. Thus the Goddess finally appears "naked" to him, riding the lion of his beastly nature, as in one of those many artistic renderings of the Goddess out of the ancient and classical pasts[11]:

> *Your naked feet upon my scarred shoulders*
> *Your eyes naked with love,*
> *Are all the gifts my beasthood can approve.*

    It is precisely this readiness, in the face of all deterrents, to *continue* to think himself in a relationship with His Creatress that explains Graves's great success, by moments, in thinking himself into the Goddess's order, however darkly problematic his expression of that order often appears to be. One may, indeed, speak in connection with his more successful efforts of an extraordinary *congruity* between his own consciousness and the mythical material he is proclaiming. In making his own individual approach to the Goddess's world, it almost seems at times as if the ancient material comes to meet Graves's efforts independently. Nowhere is this more dramatically so than where his efforts to reach out to the Goddess bring on *pictorial* manifestations: pictures of the Goddess that, as in "The White Goddess" and in "To Juan", suddenly appear out of their own inner Imaginative space—as if independent manifestations of a living Being:

> *Whose broad high brow was white as any leper's,*
> *Whose eyes were blue, with rowan-berried lips,*
> *With hair curled honey-coloured to white hips.*
>
> *She in her left hand bears a leafy quince;*
> *When with her right she crooks a finger, smiling,*
> *How may the King hold back?*
>
> *Her brow was creamy as the crested wave,*
> *Her sea-grey eyes were wild,*
> *But nothing promised that is not performed.*

    As a poet certainly, Graves greatly challenges our readiness and ability to think ourselves into a cosmological otherworld, *in the first instance by virtue of his evocations of the Goddess's direct presence.* There are not only the instances from the centrepiece-poems—"To Juan" and "The White Goddess"—from which I have cited. In "The Intrusion", for example, the poet happens unexpectedly upon his beloved who, unaware of her beholding lover, betrays a form of absorption in herself that opens out on an extraordinary dimension. The poet is overcome—his "scalp crawls" and his "eyes prick at sight"[12]

> *Of her white motionless face and folded hands*
> *Framed in such thunderclouds of sorrow...*

The beloved is herself overcome by the influence that has taken hold of her; the emphatic touches in "motionless" and "thunderclouds" are enough to intimate the *otherworldly* influence under which she herself is struggling. This influence is then identified in terms of a *mythical* image, associated with the Goddess's freedom to define the limits of any effort that is made to partake in Her world:

> *This is the dark edge of her double-axe:*
> *Divine mourning for what cannot be.*

The lovers have been judged to be presently unworthy of any fuller stability in Her world, but they have nevertheless been directly marked by Her involvement in their effort. That effort has been, and is, at least successful to this point: that the Goddess *has* been directly involved. The poet will not pretend to alter this state of things, by aspiring to a more successful showing or by seeking to win his beloved over more securely to their mutually engaged faith, because it is presently how the Goddess has judged them, what *She* has made of their effort, while Her immediate involvement in expressing this judgment about them is, or should be, enough to convince *us* that what mutually engages the lovers does have the foundation in reality the poet has assumed.[13]

The shift to the mythical image in "Intrusion" follows *from* the experience of the Goddess's direct presence, which the poet and the beloved are sharing. This will alert us to the way Graves's images often operate where there is no such indication of a direct personal experience: for example where, crystallizing the Goddess in Her dark dreadful claim on him, he speaks of

> *Honey from her lips, blood from her shadowy hand*

or where, as Her bound servant, he appears in the image of the sea-horse with

> *Under his horny ribs a blood-red stain*

or as the lion whom the Goddess rides:

> *Your naked feet upon my scarred shoulders*

Here the personal and the mythical dimensions have merged; the images come to us implicitly *bound up with* Graves's direct personal experience of the Goddess; they are not just poetically or dramatically "worked up". So too, we may suppose, in the case of other images that seem to come without prompting from the immediate situation:

> *She in her left hand bears a leafy quince;*
> *When with her right she crooks a finger, smiling,*

> *Whose broad high brow was white as any leper's,*

> *Her sea-grey eyes were wild,*

I have called attention to the way these mythical images seem to come of their own accord and from their own dimension, as if independently of Graves's conscious intention, as if they had, that is, their own intrinsic value in relation to the personal experience he is having. If so, they are not then to be discounted as "merely" mythical, or metaphorical. They seem rather to represent the pictorial *equivalent* of that which is being projected *out* of that otherworldly order into which Graves has succeeded in personally penetrating.

II

Accounts of the mythical process contemporary with Graves, even in their most radical expressions, never go as far as to proclaim the immediate possibility of recovering the mythical world in the extraordinary form Graves's production attests to. This is so even in the case of Mircea Eliade, with whose accounts one may note the closest similarities in tendency. Eliade himself focuses on gods and the "Supernaturals" generally, rather than on the Goddess, but in Eliade also there is, seemingly, complete literalness in the approach to myth, so that we find in treatments of his work the very same rationally-justified, astounded critique as was levelled at Graves:

> *What sort of scholar would talk with apparent credulity about the Creation as if it really happened, about some myths 'participating' in others, about the gods as if they really worked* **in illo tempore***, about myths as if they really arose in moments of actual release from history and sacramentally produced such moments for their devotees?*[14]

Eliade himself can attest to the experience, through myth, of "an encounter with a transhumant reality—which gives birth to the idea that something *really exists*"[15], and it is, moreover, in his view, "through the objects of this present world" that "one perceives traces of the Beings and powers of another world."[16] However, it is also clear that Eliade attributes that experience *strictly* to "[t]he man of the societies in which myth is a living thing"[17], or, as he puts it famously, "the man of the archaic societies"[18], who thrived in the remote past. Out of *that* context Eliade brings forward his ultimate view of a World that literally "'speaks' to man", and that "to understand [that World's] language [man] needs only to know the myths and decipher the symbols."[19] All of these descriptions *could* apply to Graves's own experience, except that nowhere does Eliade assume the possibility of such an experience in the modern present. On the contrary, that present is defined by Eliade as, uniquely, a time of deep historical subjection, cut off as it is from all the advantages of transcendence that derive from mythical experience, as these were formerly available to archaic man.

For Eliade—as indeed for all of the great artists and thinkers of his time[20], the modern present involves us in a world that, in its very nature, is metaphysically inconsequential, defined (to quote his own Camusian turn of phrase) principally by that temporal rhythm "in which we are condemned to live and work".[21] Misfortune and death in that context become themselves "absurd"[22], and Eliade has been seen as resorting, in his response to that condition, to the classic attitude of his own Mioritic hero of folk tradition. He imposes a meaning on the absurd by viewing the tragedy of the modern age not "as a personal historical event but as a sacramental mystery"[23], a low-point, as it were, of "Chaos" that *must* be "followed by a new Creation", of a sort that can eventually be "homologized with a cosmogony".[24] Eliade is already pointing the way to that cosmogony through his own "nostalgia" for the archaic.[25] In the meantime, he could recognize, especially in the area of modern literature, "a revolt against historical time",[26] and especially against what he alludes to as "certain contemporary philosophies of despair".[27] That revolt is achieved paradoxically through the creation of closed, hermetic universes—Eliade cites the pre-eminent case of *Finnegan's Wake* by Joyce. These "cannot be entered except by overcoming immense difficulties, like the initiatory ordeals of the archaic and traditional societies."[28] In this way the opportunity for a new "initiatory gnosis" is created that is built up from the "ruins and enigmas" of modern existence—the Waste Land, so to speak—that Eliade sees as the first phase in the return to cosmogony. No doubt he would have seen in Graves's own work some "initiatory gnosis" of the sort, especially in the case of Graves's monumental prose work, *The White Goddess*, which T.S. Eliot described as a "monstrous, stupefying, indescribable book"—echoing his earlier comments on *Finnegan's Wake* as "a monstrous masterpiece". What Eliade would *not* have allowed, however, is a possibility of recovering the mythical experience of archaic man immediately and directly in the modern present, as Graves was also claiming to do.

In fact, the modern theory of myth is almost uniformly based on an *acceptance* of our separation from the mythical experience, even where that experience *seems* to be fully grasped as a radical alternative. In the case of Ernst Cassirer, for instance, an account is offered of the nature of mythic thinking especially powerful for the way it brings out the radical kind of metaphorical *identification* mythic thinking involves. Cassirer could see very clearly that

> *for mythic thinking there is much more in metaphor than a bare "substitution", a mere rhetorical figure of speech; that what seems to our subsequent reflection as a sheer transcription is mythically conceived as a genuine and direct identification.*[29]

Were we to assume a recovery of mythic thinking in our own time, one could refer this account to the metaphors Graves himself applies to the Goddess in speaking of *the dark edge of her double-axe* or *blood from her shadowy hand*. However, like Eliade, Cassirer was elaborating on what he saw as an *archaic* mode of thinking, very distant from our own time. In contrast with that former mode, modern thinking thrives on its unique *separation* from "the hard realistic powers"[30] of the mythic image. In the modern-day production of Holderling and of Keats particularly, "the mythic power of insight breaks forth again in its full intensity and objectifying power"[31], but it does so in "the world of poetry...as a world of illusion and fantasy".[32] Cassirer sees this ultimately as "liberation", since word and mythic image are now used by the mind as "organs of its own, and [the mind] thereby recognizes them *for what they really are*: forms of its own self-revelation."[33]

From this last remark, one sees where Cassirer finally stands. It had always been for him, as he insinuates elsewhere, a matter of "the direction of the subject's interest"[34], even where it *looks* like objectivity has been conferred on the mythic process, as where he says of it:

> all spontaneity is **felt as** receptivity, all creativity as being, and every product of subjectivity **as so much** substantiality...[35]

One needs to bring out the emphasis that is implicitly made here. It was for Cassirer a necessity for humankind, in its archaic experience, to *assume* an objective presence behind its mythical invention, for only in that way could an idealization of spiritual reality be conceived that would justify all future expression of the human spirit and its ever-progressive elaboration; thus

> the Word **has** to be conceived, in the mythic mode, as a substantive being and power, before it can be comprehended as an ideal instrument, an organon of the mind, and as a fundamental function in the construction and development of spiritual reality.[36]

In this way mythic thinking is finally rationalized to fit in fully with our modern experience, and it is in the spirit ultimately of a *modern* teleology, in diametric contrast with Eliade's direction, that Cassirer involves us in his extraordinary accounts of the power of mythic identification, paradoxically among the most aesthetically satisfying formulations we have.[37] The effect is ambiguous to the point where we can speak of a philosophical *tour de force*. Cassirer continues to the end to insist on the radical uniqueness of mythic thinking, but from a point of view that, paradoxically, affirms his and our hard-earned separation and freedom from its peculiarly captive mode of operating.

◆   ◆   ◆

Like Cassirer, Owen Barfield also welcomed our necessary freedom from the phenomenal experience with which archaic man originally identified both at the level of the mythic image and of the word. It was part of *his* view, however, that what archaic man was about was not just mythical invention:

> *Men do not invent those mysterious relations between separate external objects, and between objects and feelings or ideas…The language of primitive man reports them as direct perceptual experience.*[38]

It was Barfield's special purpose (at a time contemporary with Cassirer) to claim that *originally* an objective presence does indeed lie behind the mythic image. This view is at the basis of his statement that "Mythology is the ghost of concrete meaning."[39] Barfield grounded this view on an elaborate etymological approach to the history of words, from which we gather that archaic man *must* have been involved in the phenomena, and in the representation of the phenomena, in the direct way Barfield describes:

> *you may imply, if you choose…that the earliest words in use were 'the names of sensible, material objects' and nothing more; only, in that case, you must suppose the 'sensible objects' themselves to have been something more; you must suppose that they were not, as they appear to be at present, isolated or detached from thinking and feeling.*[40]

Archaic representation involves, in fact, a whole *different* figuration, one that reflects "an awareness which we no longer have, of *an extra-sensory link* between the percipient and the representations."[41] Such a link (referred to 'mana' or 'waken') is "anterior to the individuality of [both] persons and objects"[42]—it presupposes originally "experiencing the phenomena [themselves] as representations"[43]. On that basis Barfield fills out the corollary understanding, that "This extra-sensory participation of the percipient in the representation involves a similar link between the representations themselves and of course between one percipient and another."[44] Barfield, quoting Durkheim, takes it still farther back to

> *collective mental states of extreme emotional intensity, in which representation is as yet undifferentiated from the movements and actions which make the communion towards which it tends a reality to the group. Their participation in it is so effectively lived that it is not yet properly imagined.*[45]

Like Cassirer, Barfield sees a long progression in freedom from these phenomenally captive origins. We have, in the meantime, separated out from this experience, and a concomitant of the process has been that the phenomena themselves have detached from the original element in which both humankind and the phenomena were at one time involved. Thus,

> *As consciousness develops into self-consciousness, the [now] remembered phenomena become detached and liberated from their originals and so, as images, are in some measure at man's disposal.*[46]

From here Barfield plots out two courses. On the one hand, there is the direction of modern-day science, which today dictates experiencing the phenomena "non-representationally, as objects in their own right, existing independently of human consciousness".[47] This leads to the idea of the manipulation of nature as just so many objects, to be tossed about at will, and to what Barfield calls "idolatry", "involving in the end the elimination of those last vestiges of original participation, which...survive [even] in our language".[48] There is, however, another direction that follows, from understanding that, as humankind was *once* involved (without its will) in the phenomena, so (on the basis of freedom) it can be *again*. This leads to the equally extraordinary idea—at the other extreme from scientific manipulation—of a new Creation in which "man himself now stands in a 'directionally creator relation'"[49] to the phenomena.

Something of *this* direction is already suggested, Barfield claims, in a "high" or "prophetic" art, in those instances where "a real analogy" is pursued "between metaphorical usage and original participation".[50] However, one is only able to *build* on this analogy

> *if, but only if, we admit that in the course of the earth's history, something like a Divine Word has been gradually clothing itself with the humanity it first gradually created— so that what was first spoken by God may eventually be respoken by man.*[51]

And for this to be the case, Nature, and not my own fancy, must be my representation, for then,

> *I know that what so stands is not my poor temporal personality, but the Divine Name in the unfathomable depths behind it. And if I strive to produce a work of art, I cannot then do otherwise than strive humbly to create more nearly as that creates.*[52]

Barfield thus brings us back, ultimately, to a cosmogony that would open the door for someone like Graves to find acceptance for the relationship to Nature that *he* claimed, except that what Barfield had in mind was a creative direction that was but "rudimentary as yet" and "mainly impulsive so far".[53] It is unlikely that he would have seen even in Graves's extraordinary output evidence of the "final" participation Barfield could look forward to. In the meantime, the creation of poetry, though implicitly *involved* in such a prospect, would seem to continue to import our present distance from it:

> *For it is the peculiarity of metaphorical language that, at first sight, it does often resemble very closely the language of participation; though upon closer examination its existence is seen to depend precisely on the absence of participation.*[54]

It was as far as the modern theory of myth would go to support Graves in his claim.

◆   ◆   ◆

There was, what's more, to be direct *opposition* to Graves's claim, from another area of the modern theory of myth, where the science of psychoanalysis comes into it. That Graves's poetic creation was centred in the Goddess made complete sense in the natural-cosmological terms of myth, but all that had, in turn, been fully rationalized by the psychoanalysis that confidently proclaimed these terms mere projections of the unconscious. In the natural-cosmological terms in which Graves pursues his production, as we have seen, to embrace death, as the Solar King embraces death, is to embrace the power to return from death; a goal that psychoanalysis could easily refer to the need in every man to sublimate an unconscious desire for incest with the Mother. As Jung explains:

> *sun myths and rebirth myths devise every conceivable kind of mother-analogy for the purpose of canalizing the libido into new forms and effectively preventing it from regressing to actual incest.*[55]

Freud and Jung could also explain Graves's emphasis on the darker problematic aspect of the Goddess and Her Creation and why it *must* figure in his representation, for the Mother has the power both to give and to take away, as Randall Jarrell was especially intent on pointing out:

> *That all affect, libido, mana should be concentrated in this one figure of the Mother-Muse; that love and sexuality should be inseparably intermingled with fear, violence, destruction in this "female spider"—that the loved one should be, necessarily, the Bad Mother who, necessarily, deserts and destroys the child; that the child should permit against her no conscious aggression of any kind, and intend his **cruel, capricious, incontinent**, his **bitch, vixen, hag**, to be neither condemnation nor invective, but only fascinated description of the loved and worshiped Mother and Goddess, She-Who-Must-be-Obeyed—all this is very interesting and very unoriginal. One encounters a rigorous, profound, and quite unparalleled understanding of such cases as Graves's in the many volumes of Freud…[and]…in Volume VII of Jung's* **Collected Works**, *in the second part of the essay entitled "The Relations between the Ego and the Unconscious".*[56]

Even the 'objectivity' that could be claimed for the independent power of Graves's images, seeming as they do to come from an otherworld of their own accord, is accounted for, in the psychoanalytic view, by the nature of the "archetypes" that offer themselves as "analogies" to the instinctual processes, for

> *The archetypes are the numinous, structural elements of the psyche **and possess a certain autonomy** and specific energy which enables them to attract out of the conscious mind those contents which are best suited to themselves.*[57]

The *individual* archetypal symbol—whether sea-horse, or subjected lion, or even the bloody hand of Graves's Goddess—according to Jung

> *carries conviction and at the same time expresses the content of that conviction. It is able to do this because of the numen, the specific energy stored up in the archetype.*[58]

Not that the creation of these analogies does not constitute

> *a serious problem because, as we have said, they must be ideas which attract the libido.*[59]

Hence, the tremendous significance Jung attaches to the creative fantasy, which

> *is continually engaged in producing analogies to instinctual processes in order to free the libido from sheer instinctuality by guiding it towards analogical ideas.*[60]

In the end such creation, according to Jung, will also *necessarily* produce faith, for

> *Experience of the archetype is not only impressive, it seizes and possesses the whole personality, and is naturally productive of faith.*[61]

No less than Jung was Joseph Campbell ready to allow for the psychic inevitability of the initiatory images that were formerly supplied from myth. So much so that without the supports from myth, these images must be reproduced in dream, for the same reason that Jung cites, that otherwise there could only be instinctual regression:

> *Apparently there is something in these initiatory images so necessary to the psyche that if they are not supplied from without, through myth and ritual, they will have to be announced again, through dream from within—lest our energies should remain locked in a banal, long-outmoded toyroom, at the bottom of the sea…the ageless initiation symbolism is produced spontaneously by the patient himself at the moment of the release.*[62]

It was *also* Campbell's view, however, that a crucial distinction would have to be introduced between the *sources* of dream and those of myth (a view that is paralleled in the distinction Graves introduces between poems and dreams[63]):

> *But if we are to grasp the full value of the materials, we must note that myths are not exactly comparable to dream…*
>
> *we are in the presence rather of immense consciousness than of darkness…*
>
> *And so, to grasp the full value of the mythological figures that have come down to us, we must understand that they are not only the symptoms of the unconscious (as indeed are all human thoughts and acts) but also* **controlled and intended statements** *of certain spiritual principles…*[64]

On the basis of his own vast research into these mythological figures and materials, Campbell could bring himself to the point of formulating the one great principle that underlies them all:

> *Briefly formulated, the universal doctrine teaches that all the visible structures of the world—all* **things** *and beings—are the effects of a ubiquitous* **power** *out of which they rise, which supports and fills them during the period of their manifestation, and back into which they must ultimately dissolve.*[65]

One notes of Campbell's emphasis in this passage the focus on "all *things* and beings" that are "the effects" of this "ubiquitous power". *Objectivity* is, in this way, restored to the mythical process. And it is in this spirit that Campbell throws himself into his own engagement with the mythical experience. It takes a form here that might lead one to suppose it was Graves himself who is speaking:

> *the meeting with the goddess (who is incarnate in every woman) is the final test of the talent of the hero to win the boon of love (charity:* **amor fati***), which is life itself enjoyed as the encasement of eternity…*[66]*…the goddess is red with the fire of life; the earth, the solar system, the galaxies of far-existing space, all swell within her womb. For she is the world creatrix, ever-mother, ever-virgin. She encompasses*

> *the encompassing, nourishes the nourishing, and is the life of everything that lives. She is also the death of everything that dies. The whole round of existence is accomplished within her sway, from birth, through adolescence, maturity, and senescence, to the grave. She is the womb and the tomb: the sow that eats her farrow. Thus she unites the "good" and the "bad", exhibiting the two modes of the remembered mother, **not as personal only, but as universal**. The devotee is expected to contemplate the two with equal equanimity. Through this exercise his spirit is purged of its infantile, inappropriate sentimentalities and resentments, and his mind opened to the inscrutable presence which exists, not primarily as "good" and "bad" with respect to his childlike human convenience, his weal and woe, but as the law and image of the nature of being.*[67]

At another point, Campbell will describe it as a passage

> *from the infantile illusions of "good" and "evil" to an experience of the majesty of cosmic law, purged of hope and fear, and at peace in the understanding of the revelation of being.*[68]

Here, we will feel, is all the confirming support Graves would have needed, for like him Campbell assumes that is it both possible and imperative to recover the mythical experience now. Campbell was pursuing his own view at this time altogether independently of Graves, who had published *The White Goddess* only a year before Campbell brought out *Hero with a Thousand Faces* (from which these excerpts are taken.) The concurrence is extraordinary and might have given pause to Jarrell when he brought forward his critique of Graves some seven or eight years later. An entirely independent case had been made for the objectivity of the process that Jarrell, following Jung, had preconcluded to be purely subjective. In fact, with Campbell, as with Graves, it is precisely the point that the psychoanalytic patient must learn to transcend his own personal situation by entering fully into the universal process. (For Graves it is the poet's task to lead him there.) Then he would see that the "good" and the "bad" that so obsess and tie down his mind, and that are the basis of his "hope" and "fear", arise as the principles upon which the order of Nature itself is founded. Unity, if anywhere, will be found there. This was already understood in the Romantic context out of which Graves was writing: "fear" (in "To Juan") is ultimately subsumed in "love". It is how Wordsworth himself presents it, who also saw it as a case of refusing the regression back to death; only in Wordsworth, it is the universal forms of Nature that assure his passage through:

> [I] *rather did with jealousy shrink back*
> *From every combination that might aid*
> *The tendency, too potent in itself,*
> *Of habit to enslave the mind, I mean*
> *Oppress it by the laws of vulgar sense,*
> *And substitute a universe of death,*
> *The falsest of all worlds, in place of that*
> *Which is divine and true. To fear and love,*
> *To love, as first and chief, for there fear ends,*
> *Be this ascribed; to early intercourse,*
> *In presence of sublime and lovely Forms,*
> *With the adverse principles of pain and joy,*
> *Evil, as one is rashly named by those*
> *Who know not what they say. From love, for here*
> *Do we begin and end, all grandeur comes,*
> *All truth and beauty, from pervading love,*
> *That gone, we are as dust.*[69]

Campbell himself assumes an ultimate peace from the unity of the two experiences as these come together in the Mothering Goddess:

> *She was Cosmic Power, the totality of the universe, the harmonization of all the pairs of opposites, combining wonderfully the terror of absolute destruction with an impersonal yet motherly reassurance.*[70]

Likewise, in "To Juan" as we have seen, Graves assumes an ultimate unity, but in him the duality persists, if only because *he* was working this experience out immediately and directly through the form of being he saw himself as having at that moment. Hence the persistence in *his* representations of the Goddess of the dual aspect of Her involvement with him. It was in any case Graves's view (at least for the longest time; there would be a further evolution in his view towards the end of his career[71]) that man had always been and would have to remain in a dualistic relationship with his Creatress, for

Man is a demi-god: he always has either one foot or the other in the grave; woman is divine because she can keep both her feet always in the same place, whether in the sky, in the underworld, or on this earth. Man envies her and tells himself lies about his own completeness, and thereby makes himself miserable; because if he is divine she is not even a demi-goddess—she is mere nymph and his love for her turns to scorn and hate.[72]

III

What are we to make, then, of the insistent efforts of Campbell and Graves to announce the prospect of a new mythical experience in the modern world, one founded on the basis of Nature, in defiance of the rigidly qualifying strictures of the many acknowledged modern theorists of myth? In Graves's view, inability, or unwillingness, to recognize that the time was ripe for a fresh breakthrough into mythical experience has a clear historical explanation. It is the end-result of an intellectual pretension to resolve the almost intolerable duality in which man is naturally placed, by which he has, over centuries, rationalized himself outside the sphere of Nature, and so outside the Goddess's order.[73] Referring himself directly to the mythical record, Graves put it as follows:

> [man] *is divine not in his single person but in his twinhood. As Osiris, the Spirit of the Waxing Year, he is always jealous of the weird, Set, the Spirit of the Waning Year, and vice-versa; he cannot be both of them at once except by an intellectual effort that destroys his humanity, and this is the fundamental defect of the Apollonian or Jehovistic cult.*[74]

By this "cult" Graves had in mind the longstanding effects of the decisive intervention over the course of the 1st millennium B.C. of patriarchal influences that had been slowly seeping into both the Hellenic and Hebraic cultures, from which our own Western experience derives. War had been declared in Heaven with the conflict between Jehovah and the Great Goddess of 7th century B.C. Jerusalem, which led to Her displacement by this Universal God, and

> [t]*he result of envisaging this God of pure meditation, the Universal Mind still premised by the most reputable modern philosophers, and enthroning him above Nature as essential Truth and Goodness was not an altogether happy one.*[75]
>
> *Then came the early Greek philosophers who were strongly opposed to magical poetry as threatening their new religion of logic, and under their influence a rational poetic language (now called the Classical) was elaborated in honour of their*

*patron Apollo and imposed on the world as the last word in spiritual illumination.*⁷⁶

Not that the elaborate, withering indictment of Western tradition that we get from Graves in *The White Goddess* does not still leave him with the challenge of effectively harnessing the energy associated with his engagement with the Goddess. For without a deliberate, conscious reining of this energy, the need for which Graves himself acknowledges, there is the real danger of being destroyed by it, as Graves's poems themselves bear witness.⁷⁷ The purpose of the post-Exilic religious reformation that substituted Jehovah for the Goddess had been precisely to disassociate man from the destructive influence of his commitment to the 'darker' side of the Goddess's claims on him. Thus a recent reader of Graves, considering the challenge of this crucial opposition, between the "voracious life-giving energy" on the one hand and "the rationalizing element" on the other, concludes:

> *the issue is how successfully the two key elements can be accommodated without the energy being destroyed.*⁷⁸

One keeps this universal energy of Nature under control, according to this reader, "through mythic or religious ritual".⁷⁹ Ted Hughes, a modern poet whom one should be linking with Graves, is further recruited on behalf of this view.⁸⁰ However, it is truer to say that this force of mythic or religious ritual, if it is effective, must *by its own operation* control the energy. We have an especially powerful instance of the operation of this force (of mythic ritual) in Graves's poem, "She Is No Liar":

> *She is no liar, yet she will wash away*
> *Honey from her lips, blood from her shadowy hand,*
> *And, dressed at dawn in clean white robes will say,*
> *Trusting the ignorant world to understand:*
> *'Such things no longer are; this is today.'*

◆   ◆   ◆

"Such things no longer are;"—Graves's view was that modern man had come into a new age in which all that had formerly obstructed the Goddess's power to direct his life had been left behind. Graves's faith that this was so was categorical, and the situation could not be reversed for him.

With a characteristic freedom from the effects of history, he could say with complete assurance and with a complete finality, in "The End of Play":

> *We have reached the end of pastime...*
> ....
> *We have at last ceased idling...*
> ....
> *We tell no lies now, at last cannot be*
> *The rogues we were—so evilly linked in sense*
> *With what we scrutinized...*[81]

One is astounded by the unitary view Graves takes of history, which allowed him to affirm this faith and to install himself, very simply, without any further sense of any conflict that might subvert or continue to wear away at his vision.[82] It is the measure of a formidable single-mindedness in Graves that in this view he stands perhaps alone.[83] All had been for him a matter of the suppression merely of the Goddess-culture, which had remained inexpungeable and irrepressible, so that it was only a matter of time before that culture would openly affirm itself again. Hence the account of his purposes as Graves shared this with his audience in his 1957 Y.M.H.A. lecture:

> *It is enough for me to quote the myths and give them historical sense: tracing a certain faith through its historical vicissitudes—from where it was paramount, to when it has been driven underground and preserved by witches, travelling minstrels, remote country-folk and a few secret heretics to the newly established religion.*[84]

This faith had been restored again in the twentieth century principally through Graves himself, though Graves further cites, as indirect evidence, the fact that the Virgin Mary could now in the established religions "legitimately be saluted as 'the Queen of Heaven'—the very title borne by Rahab (the Goddess Astarte), against whom the prophet Jeremiah declaimed in the name of his monotheistic Father-god Jehovah."[85]

Graves's assurance in proclaiming this faith is in large part a feature of its surviving power as he saw this operating especially in British culture. Thus he emphasizes that "the Queen of Heaven with her retinue of female saints had a far greater hold in the popular imagination between the Crusades and the Civil War than either the Father or the Son."[86] This Thunder-God, as Graves presents Him, did get re-instated at the time of the Puritan Revolution in England, but it is characteristic of Graves that he sees this God's triumph as "short-lived"; it could never have withstood "the stubborn conviction" among the British that Britain was "a Mother Country, not a Father-land".[87] Writing out of this view as well as the power of his own experience, Graves has simply no inclination to consider that perhaps Western civilization as a whole had been through a deeper conflict and a deeper agony. However, Ted Hughes, who was (up to a point) a professed disciple of Graves, took a very different view of the matter in his book, *Shakespeare and the Goddess of Complete Being*. There it is Hughes's special insistence that man *continues* in conflict with himself over the Goddess, and no one saw that this would be so with greater clarity than did Shakespeare, whose case *about* the conflict, according to Hughes, has still to be heard—through his plays.[88] It is the conflict of the Reformation itself, behind which Hughes, like Graves, sees the conflict of Jehovah and the great Goddess of 7th century B.C. Jerusalem.[89] It is, according to Hughes, the *one* conflict in which Shakespeare is engaged from the beginning of his career to its end.

Macbeth, for Hughes, is the play in which this conflict comes to fullest expression, being also the turning point in Shakespeare's own dealings with it. In his earlier tragedies, including *Hamlet* and *King Lear*, Shakespeare had already dramatized the process by which his heroes suddenly succumb to the "delusion"[90] of thinking their beloved ones unholy. In this they pretend to do *without* the Goddess's all-supporting life by charging *Her*, as it were, with dark and unholy motives. Now, in *Macbeth*, the nature of this charge is fully exposed, for the erroneous "Tarquinian" madness that it represents, for which the hero must be destroyed. It is the hero's rational "Adonis" world of "Puritan-style ideals"[91]—which underlies that madness—that must be destroyed, by the irrepressible life of the Goddess. Macbeth's real crime in this respect precedes his appearance in the play and is the measure of his value as a representation of the more recent Shakespearean tragic heroes who precede him. Macbeth must be set right by being driven to destroy his Adonis-nature, murdering Duncan and seeking to murder Banquo in the process, only because all are guilty of rejecting the Goddess. However, up to that point Shakespeare's heroes have *thought* themselves justified in their charge, and it is the power that this thought exercises over them that so impresses Hughes and (so Hughes supposes) Shakespeare:

> *Even after it has been capsized in spectacular fashion by that irrational secret-sharer [Tarquin] rising from beneath it, that point of view, of the Adonis ego, though it no longer has any*

control over its actions, always retains the ability, like a ship's gimbal, to think itself rational (at least, it does so up to the point at which the ego is destroyed, and a new self, neither Adonis nor Tarquin, emerges—as begins to happen in **King Lear***).*

It is Hughes's argument that Western man continues to lie somewhere in the general area in which Shakespeare's tragic heroes find themselves before *Macbeth* comes through to set right all delusion. The challenge for Hughes lies in the fact that rational man must learn to see him*self* in Macbeth and indeed in every Shakespearean tragic hero who comes before him. Shakespeare had given direct and complete expression to Western man's judgment of the Goddess, only to bring out, in fact, the *tragedy* in that judgment:

> *What Shakespeare* **goes on** *to reveal is that in destroying her* [the Goddess] *he destroys himself and brings down Heaven and Earth in ruins.*[92]

But this is, for Hughes in any case

> *the inevitable crime of Civilization, or even the inevitable crime of consciousness.*[93] *Certainly the crime of the Reformation—the "offense/From Luther until now/That has driven a culture mad" as Auden phrased it.*[94]

But what if this sudden shift in consciousness in the hero, into judgment, turned out *not* to be some misguided "offense" stemming from a "delusion", whether this is seen as criminal or tragic (which is to say, in the latter case, stemming from "error"), but a new *objective* development, which Shakespeare took that seriously because it seemed to him it *had* become the reality. Everything *had*, disastrously, fallen apart, and all because the kind of "love" Shakespeare's tragic hero had known with his beloved *had* failed and a new perception of the extent of human depravity come into view. If this is so, the story would not then be (as it appears to be on the surface) about "rejection of the Female" or "the Puritan fear of female sexuality", but about some still *deeper* failure or change, something still *more* to reckon with than either Graves or Hughes seemed ready to acknowledge: a matter of coming to terms with a deeper degree of depravity than we had supposed ourselves subject to and that could, therefore, potentially only confound us the more. This is to shift the focus I have been pursuing thus far into a still more problematic depth—"fear", as in the case of Macbeth, originating, in this conception, from a deeper instability and a deeper derangement. I shall thereby be raising a still *further* issue that would seem to arise from the course Western experience has taken, which throws into doubt whether Graves's (and Hughes's) conception of "love" and of the "Female" or Goddess takes us far enough or as far as we need to take ourselves, if we are to avoid any deeper subversion than what Hughes claimed has characterized Western experience thus far.[95]

II

THE WORST OF DEPRAVITY

I

For, what shall we say *is* Macbeth's "fear" and *what* the violence of conception that takes him over, to the point where, it would seem, he has *no choice but* to yield?

> ***why*** *do I yield to that suggestion*
> *Whose horrid image doth unfix my hair*
> *And make my seated heart knock at my ribs*
> *Against the use of nature?*

Hughes and Graves would have us believe that this is the Goddess taking Macbeth over, possessing him in order to avenge Herself against him for the crime he has committed against Her.[96] Macbeth's crime lies in rejecting the Goddess by turning away from Her sensual creation, for which *he* has judged Her unholy. But does Macbeth, when viewed more closely, represent the *judgment* of sensuality, or does he not rather represent the complete *indulgence* of it, along with Lady Macbeth, and indeed all the characters in this play, with whom he is united in a complete sensual ambition? To what extent all are immersed in the darkest sensuality in *Macbeth* can be gleaned from what James Calderwood has to say about the opening battle scene in which a universal ambition is drastically played out:

> *As priestly leaders of the royal forces Macbeth and Banquo preside over a ceremony in which the Scots are purged and exalted by the shedding of sacred blood in the King's cause even as mankind was once purged by the shedding of Christ's sacred blood on Golgotha. Only men in battle who bathe in their own and their enemies' blood, are able to partake bodily and symbolically in the divinity of the state. As Christ's blood streaming in the firmament offers everlasting life to the worshiper, so the sacred blood of battle yields immortality to Macbeth and Banquo as Bellona's deathless bridegrooms and as participants in the greater life of the state (Macbeth will be king, Banquo will beget kings).*[97]

We are, with *Macbeth*, in a world that, in its original situation—before the tragic breakdown—is, in fact, complete as perhaps no other is in Shakespeare. It is a complete world because of the *grounds* of its justification, archaic as those grounds certainly are, involving human nature as they do in the complete depth of its violent sensuality. From *this* starting position (in itself an extraordinary feat of cultural anamnesis on Shakespeare's part) Shakespeare had a point to make, as we shall see. As Calderwood explains, war is intrinsic to this archaic world, being literally its means of divination and of sanctification, for,

> *It enables kings to look into the entrails of violence and see if they are still sacred to the gods*[98]

The Challenger in this world is thus the King's necessary and welcome counterpart, since *he* raises, by his own daring rebellion, the issue of the king's sacredness, which must be continually justified anew, and in this sense

> *each fight with a challenger who would kill him is a test of the king's sacredness: will the golden bough remain on its branch? Will the god's strange heart still beat within him?*[99]

The seemingly complete extent of the violence, as we have it in *Macbeth*, represents the fullest measure of that justification. In fact, so complete is the violence at a certain point we are *un*able to distinguish the king's challenger from his defender. As Calderwood puts it, "it is a scene of undifferentiated brutality" for "all are bloodily one in battle".[100] But this is as it ideally should be, for only out of the deepest engagement in these terms—the deepest violence and the deepest effort of will on both sides, will justification come. Thus in the context of this battle

> *violence erodes cultural distinctions, even the fundamental distinction between "us" and "them", yet its function is to reaffirm and recreate distinctions by singling out, not scapegoat victims, but heroic survivors.*[101]

For in this context, "surviving is a sacred achievement".[102]

It is the chief value of the warrior in this world that he can survive this scene of battle, as Macbeth and Banquo survive it, and in doing so justify himself. The king's justification thus follows from the warrior's own. If the warrior is happy to serve his king, this is because, as Harry Berger Jr. points out, it is the king who provides him with the "bloody occasions"—and so "the reputation and honors" that follow from success on those "occasions"—by which the warrior seeks to prove and to justify himself.¹⁰³ It is easy to see, at the same time, the constant threat that might be posed to the king by the pride of the warrior on whose extreme prowess the king must rely for his justification.¹⁰⁴ We can see how ideas of service and love would then enter into this context, to safeguard against overweening pride, and as it were to sublimate the threat of violence. It was the view of Johannes Huizinga that these ideas come into play in the time of the Middle Ages (in which Shakespeare's action is set) as a purely formal code of conventions, deliberately constructed and imposed on a tendency to ferocious passion that is everywhere present at that time because of its reigning quality of pride.¹⁰⁵ Thus

> *Love has to be elevated to the height of a rite. The overflowing violence of passion demands it. Only by constructing a system of forms and rules for the violent emotions can barbarity be escaped.*¹⁰⁶

> *The passionate and violent soul of the age...could not dispense with the severest rules and the strictest formalism. All emotions required a rigid system of conventional forms, for without them passion and ferocity would have made havoc of life.*¹⁰⁷

And so we may approach those extraordinary moments in Shakespeare's play when Macbeth and Lady Macbeth formally express their obeisance to Duncan in spite of the extreme achievement that Macbeth has displayed in battle that seems to redound more to his own honor:

> Duncan. *O worthiest cousin!*
> *The sin of my ingratitude even now*
> *Was heavy upon me: thou art so far before,*
> *That swiftest wing of recompense is slow*
> *To overtake thee. Would thou hadst less deserved,*
> *That the proportion both of thanks and payment*
> *Might have been mine! only I have left to say,*
> *More is thy due than more than all can pay.*

> Macbeth. *The service and the loyalty I owe,*
> *In doing it, pays itself. Your highness' part*
> *Is to receive our duties: and our duties*
> *Are to your throne and state children and servants;*
> *Which do but what they should, by doing every thing*

Safe toward your love and honour.

Duncan.   *Welcome hither:*
I have begun to plant thee, and will labour
To make thee full of growing.

* * *

Duncan. *See, see, our honoured hostess!*
The love that follows us sometime is our trouble,
Which still we thank as love…

Lady Macbeth.   *All our service*
In every point twice done, and then done double,
Were poor and single business to contend
Against those honours deep and broad wherewith
Your majesty loads our house: for those of old,
And the late dignities heaped up to them,
We rest your hermits.

We are setting aside for the present the effect on these moments (in the way *we* actually see them) of the "evil" intention in Macbeth and in Lady Macbeth that has *also* disturbingly penetrated this world. Here I wish to propose that the play's original experience transcends Huizinga's notion of a deliberately constructed culture, as if sentiments of love and service were for the most part, as he argues, only put on, only moving *towards* being essential, if no *less* crucial for all that.[108] On the contrary, there seems a case for saying that service and love are themselves an intrinsic part of the unified whole of the original *Macbeth*-world—as *much* a feature of what holds that world together and makes it complete, as the extreme violence on which that world is predicated. It is a logical predication, for if it *is* the extreme violence that makes the *Macbeth*-world complete—because only such violence creates the necessary basis for a complete justification—so too must the love that finally supports that justification be complete. We are to imagine an *original* condition of culture in which utmost sensual depths of dark violence are perfectly expressed and perfectly contained by the love and service that support and motivate that violence. It is what we glimpse in those moments of obeisance that unite Macbeth and Lady Macbeth in the same expression of will. These moments present the characters in the image of what they *were* until now, borne up by love and service. Only, the characters have now separated out from the reality and so give us merely the image. So too was Macbeth in battle at one time borne up by love and service, until things changed, though we are only given insight into Macbeth's love in hypocritical fashion later, in the words he uses to justify slaying Duncan's guards *after* he has murdered Duncan:

> *The expedition of my violent love*
> *Outran the pauser, reason. Here lay Duncan…*
> ……………………………………………………
> ………………………..: *who could refrain,*
> *That had a heart to love, and in that heart,*
> *Courage, to make's love known?*

Here is our glimpse into the principal original motive of this world, now gone preternaturally awry. All *was* formerly a unity—the violence and the love quite *one*, until the supporting love goes out of it. Macbeth finds himself in battle immersed in an extreme violence, fighting the King's cause suddenly *without* the love that had borne him up in his will to that point. That fact is momentously registered through the contrast with Banquo *who himself has battled no less fiercely or completely* but who comes away from his engagement as Macbeth could have expected to—supported still by love.[109] Herein lies the horror of the separation of "foul" from "fair" from the former unity in which they lay; what was "fair" and should have remained "fair", and does remain "fair" for Banquo (the "foul" being incorporated into *it* for him) has become simply "foul" for Macbeth. His complete violence of will has been released from the supporting reality of love, with the effect that, without its support and without its defense, he is now overwhelmed by the violence of his will. In this complete world, Macbeth's will has identified with the King in fighting his cause; stripped now of any further underlying motive of love, Macbeth *becomes* in his will the very King with whom he is identified in his defense. His very identity has gone over to *being* King, and he meets the recognition from the Witches that this is so with fear because in that moment for the first time he consciously recognizes that this is so. His displacement of Duncan as King has already taken place and so *must* lead to murder.

What Calderwood's account overlooks is that the situation in *Macbeth* has altered—preternaturally so, so that we view all that we are given in the beginning of the play as it were in double form. We see on the one hand what the *Macbeth*-world is originally constituted of and at the same time measure a seismic alteration in it, which has everything, in fact, different and looking different. That effect extends to the imagery of Golgotha that the Sergeant elaborates in his account of the battle, which does *seem* to positively identify the blood of the battling warriors with that of Christ, but *in fact* registers an effect wildly inappropriate. Calderwood himself acknowledges the association as a "grotesque collusion".[110] This is generally the case with all that is presented in the play's opening scenes. A new *difference* has come into it and to some extent come into the consciousness of all the characters who have witnessed Macbeth's action on the battlefield, though, being unused to any other world, none are in the position to recognize what that difference imports. Nevertheless, it is clearly present in the consciousness of the *effect* of Macbeth's deeds, which project him as bearing the very identity of the Rebel or Challenger with whom he has literally united in battle, and who, by this perverted route, through Macbeth, has *become* King:

> Ross. *The king hath happily received, Macbeth,*
> *The news of **thy** success: and when he reads*
> ***Thy personal venture in the rebels' fight**,*
> *His wonders and his praises do contend*
> ***Which should be thine or his**: silenced with that,*
> *In viewing o'er the rest o' the selfsame day,*
> *He finds thee in the stout Norweyan ranks,*
> *Nothing afeard of what thyself didst make,*
> ***Strange images** of death. As thick as hail*
> *Came post with post, and every one did bear*
> ***Thy** praises in his kingdom's great defence,*
> *And poured them down before him.*

Macbeth is originally identified with a form of extreme expression in violent will that has been the supporting power of his society until now while the substance of love also motivated it. The sudden *withdrawal* of this substance of love now leaves the will to operate on its own. Macbeth is suddenly left without any defense against that will, which being as extreme as the love that contained it, cannot be resisted. The human will has come free in its essential depravity, and no defense in human nature is able to protect against it. Thus the horror and the fear that overcome Macbeth who is left grappling helplessly with himself, for the utmost violence of his will is bound to overpower him. It is the measure Shakespeare has taken of the depths of human depravity; he has traced it back to this original situation when love had all in check. Then, dramatizing the moment in which the primal human will separates out from love, he shows with a perfect horror how little power human nature on its own can have over this will. To make the point with an even greater effect of horror, he then brings into his exposition diachronically the power that the *ideal* of love might still be thought to have over the will—for love has now *become* an ideal, is no longer the governing reality. This is where Macbeth imagines the angels judging his murderous intentions before he gets down to the murder. Here Shakespeare brings love back into it, with all the power it could exercise over the mind *as* an ideal, and bringing it back he demonstrates how the ideal in this case can have no power over that will. Macbeth's most evolved Imaginations of that ideal, by which his projected deed is judged, do have the effect of rousing his conscience but can have no effect in keeping him from seeing the deed through.[111]

What can Shakespeare's purpose have been in depicting this primal scene if not to cite, as evidence, the sheer extent of violent sensuality that is there deep down in the human make-up, if only as an atavistic survival today? Starting from an archaic world, which Shakespeare in his own way recovers, he shows how sensuality in this degree would *have* to be restrained by a power of love that is there originally in the same degree. He assumes, as his own mythographer of the archaic, that formerly this was so, and then deliberately takes us back, to that fateful moment when separation from love is brought about. The sensuality that had until then been kept in check now subverts disastrously from the sheer extent of its expression, its completeness. Having once subserved the "mana" of love, it is now exposed for the horrible depravity it constitutes when left to its own purposes and acts in its own right. It has the power of a pure unchecked somatic *disturbance* that can only take Macbeth away with itself in his mind.[112] This is what absorbs him in fear from the start, and what keeps him in fear throughout. And so his famous visions, which only have the *content* of moral imagination when in *substance* they are woven out of his disturbance, so that the imagination of Duncan in his virtues *must* give way to those of the daggers that rush him into the murder without impediment. Those visions continue, of course, beyond the murder, and are continually at play in Macbeth[113], until, by the sheer force of his destructive will, he manages in a sense to kill them, destroying his whole human nature in the process. In comparison with Macbeth, Lady Macbeth one might say has only "played" at being possessed, is not as fully engaged, is herself in dismay at the diabolic visions that continue in her husband.[114] She goes mad ultimately less from the influence of demonic possession than from her horror of Macbeth's complete separation from her, the only person with whom, in this world of violent debacle, she could have retained *any* form of hopeful human complicity.

II

The action in *Macbeth* is only the most extreme and the most horrid case of a tragic pattern in Shakespeare that is typical of this phase. We feel the connection back to the other tragedies especially where Macbeth and Lady Macbeth are suddenly presented to us, at the scene of the murder, in their fundamental innocence. It is the effect that so impressed John Middleton Murry:

> *That a man and woman should, in the very act of heinous and diabolical murder, reveal themselves as naïve and innocent, convulses our morality and awakens in us thoughts beyond the reaches of our souls.*[115]

Innocence is the fundamental condition of Shakespeare's tragic characters, when one compares them to the villains via whom their destinies are galvanized. Villains though they have *become*, Macbeth and Lady Macbeth are still innocent, and so tragic, and the lesson they dramatize is therefore the more horrifying because of that. Their fate is typical of the Shakespearean tragic action: innocent as they are, they are now subverted by their own sensuality, which they had *thought* love, and which was indeed love until their condition altered. The reality of sensual life has suddenly become pretension, and we see now that they are *composed* of sensuality and are judged for it. Sensuality, separated from love, turns into depravity.

The moment when this alteration takes place is the moment of evil, which strikes like lightning, immediately and with an overwhelming violence, because, at any and every cost, the separation from sensuality must now take place—for whatever evolutionary reasons we may divine. The Shakespearean villain, from this perspective, is merely party to the process, a mechanism merely who adds to the effect of the process that must now go forward. Shakespeare's tragic characters remaining, as they do, profoundly attached to the sensuality and to the love that they have known, which is the only love they *can* know, the effect of separation is world-altering; but it is now what *has* to be borne, for human sensuality can only subvert now.[116] How dismal a process this is the plays bear witness to, for Shakespeare's tragic characters remain profoundly implicated. And in this they are the image of what *we* might be if we thought ourselves into, or pretended to live out, our own sensuality, in the complete and unthinking way we might wish to.

Lear is only slightly less horrid as presentation in this respect than is *Macbeth*. Lightning strikes here in the same way—the scene altering instantaneously, and with a complete irreversibility. A love that was until then supported in its sensuality now converts, disastrously—into hate, from the influence of a sensuality now become depravity:

> *For by the sacred radiance of the sun*
> *The mysteries of Hecate, and the night;*
> *By all the operation of the orbs*
> *From whom we do exist and cease to be;*
> *Here I disclaim all my paternal care,*
> *Propinquity and property of blood,*
> *And as a stranger to my heart and me*
> *Hold thee from this forever. The barbarous Scythian*
> *Or he that makes his generation messes*
> *To gorge his appetite, shall to my bosom*
> *Be as well neighboured, pitied, and relieved,*
> *As thou my sometime daughter.*

No villain is required to help subvert things here, unless that villain might be Cordelia. It will seem outlandish to say so, but this is nevertheless in a certain sense the case. Of the perversely sensual basis of Lear's love of Cordelia there is no doubt, but to the extent that Cordelia is involved in this love, who can say that she herself does not *share* in that sensuality or express *herself* in it? Cordelia balking at the profession of her love for Lear in the ritual, from this point of view, can be seen as a deliberate effort to repress her own involvement in that sensuality, which she finds she cannot openly express herself in, from a reticence she cannot control, which itself converts to pride.[117] Evil has entered the *Lear*-world as it were through this back route. Pride of this kind can easily be seen as hate; and so Lear sees it; he sees, also, the evil at work through it, and on that basis must react in his turn, for he can only reject Cordelia for it. That reaction is repeated later when Lear sees it in Goneril:

> *Darkness and devils!*

Only, by comparison of course, Cordelia is relatively far more innocent. It is principally through Lear that the subversion by sensuality takes place and depravity is exposed. As the passage quoted above shows, the breakdown is as great, and as profoundly sensual in its turn, as the borne-up experience of love that had sustained it until this moment. But what can we imagine

Cordelia's perception of Lear to be at this moment, or of her own love shared with him up to now? As far as I know, no commentary exists on what we may suppose Cordelia is experiencing through the extensive silence that marks her response to Lear's outburst at this point. But we can surely imagine that, among other feelings, Cordelia would be wondering about the basis of the love shared with him until now, and feeling some guiltiness about it. Not in the sense that she wonders how she could love this man, but that she wonders on what grounds she herself has been having this love, since it was love partaken of *with* him. When she and Lear meet again later in the play, after much suffering, both have by then been largely purged of the sensual basis of the love that they once shared.[118]

No one is spared the judgement; I have elsewhere[119] gone in some depth into the basis of guilt also in Desdemona, after Othello himself breaks down. The sensuality that absorbs *them* from the beginning needs no elucidation, and it becomes the doorway into a view of the depravity that is thought to lurk in these characters as an essential condition—tragically so in light of how they otherwise appear to us on the surface, as perhaps Shakespeare's greatest romantic lovers. The breakdown from sensuality into depravity is overwhelmingly clear in the case of Othello, but Shakespeare's vision of fundamental depravity extends in the play, as I show, to Desdemona herself. It is a measure of the universal import of what we may call the Shakespearean doubt at this time; it is a doubt that Shakespeare had carried over to *Othello* from *Hamlet*. Human nature is seen in *Hamlet* as *determined* by lust, this being the reigning view of human nature on which Shakespeare was then acting, which he had derived from Luther.[120] Even if we feel that Shakespeare stands finally for something else, something ultimately beyond this pessimism, it would seem that he assumed this view of human nature to be fundamentally true, and it is how his characters are shown to us, after falling from their formerly protected sphere in a world where lust and a general sensuality are originally absorbed in a certain order of love. Love in the tragedies is presented by Shakespeare in those terms, and it is *this* original ordering love that now goes; when it does, the subversion by sensuality is overwhelming—virtually everyone will and must die from it, in one elaborate way or another.[121]

Hamlet's subversion by sensuality is in his mind, but the subversion is no less real for that. The picture of lust that presents itself to him from his world derives not only from what he sees in the relationship between Claudius and his mother, but also from the relationship between his mother and his father:

> *why, she would hang on him,*
> *As if increase of appetite had grown*
> *By what it fed on*:

Originally, Hamlet's picture incorporates this sensuality of his parents into an idea of their love, in keeping with the fundamental pattern of experience in Shakespeare's tragedies, and Hamlet's own love of his father is bound up with this picture. But with the Ghost's revelation about his condition in the afterlife, the lust (typically) separates out from that picture as its own force, for which his father is now suffering punishment in the otherworld.[122] His father's murder at Claudius's hands is in this respect but the image of the former's condemnation of himself, as if in his own lustful relationship to his wife lay the seeds of her further relationship to his murderer Claudius, who *is* the demonic image of himself.

Soon Hamlet is bitterly generalizing this condition of lust about everyone. If what his mother has made of herself with Claudius, or what Claudius himself represents of the grossest sensuality, so subverts Hamlet's mind, it is because they have become the images of a universal human condition that Hamlet can now see also touches him, and he is now himself subverted:

> *for virtue cannot so inoculate our old stock but we shall relish of it*
>
> *for the power of beauty will sooner transform honesty from what it is to a bawd than the force of honesty can translate beauty into his likeness: this was sometime a paradox, but now the time gives it proof.*

It is the same view of a now *altered* condition of love that Iago expounds upon at length in *Othello*, that condition being (appallingly) the natural ground for his own introduction onto this scene. Addressing a love *thus altered*, Iago can now confidently proclaim of *it*:

> *It is merely a lust of the blood and a permission of the will.*[123]

III

To return to the model put forward by Graves and by Hughes—I see a very different picture emerging from Shakespeare's presentation. An *original* picture presents itself—an original archaic world—in which love in various forms does indeed reign over all and have all in hand, and we can certainly conceive of *this* totality as expressing the Goddess's primal hold over Her indulged creation. Lust and a *general* sensuality that makes room for self-indulgence, ferocious character, and even violence—all this may be said to have had at one time an assigned place within an order principally directed by love. But then this indulgent and supporting love withdraws, and all is as if poured out, in a way that seems to confirm directly all that Luther had said[124] was true about human nature: that it is fundamentally, grossly and hopelessly depraved:

> *A serving-man, proud in heart and mind; that curled my hair; wore gloves in my cap; served the lust of my mistress' heart and did the act of darkness with her...one that slept in the contriving of lust and waked to do it...false of heart, light of ear, bloody of hand; hog in sloth, fox in stealth, wolf in greediness, dog in madness, lion in prey.*

Edgar's speech, as Poor Tom, catalogues it all. Humankind has been left to itself alone, subject to almost any subversion by its own sensuality, and with no further defense against itself, save for what it might find of support from whatever might come of this situation. If we are to speak of any further *return* to the Goddess, surely it would have to be with reference ultimately to *all* that we may suppose human nature to be composed of, as Shakespeare saw it. And, coming away from Shakespeare, it will boggle our minds to imagine the kind of confidence that would allow us the total leap in human experience that Graves for one proposed.

We may suppose that what Shakespeare thought of human nature would have some bearing on what we consider Imaginatively possible today, and Ted Hughes certainly assumed this, though I would propose a different lesson to be derived from what Shakespeare presents. The problem of our re-uniting with the Goddess necessitates for Hughes a complex evolution *with* Shakespeare, through the whole of the rest of the work that follows from his great tragedies. It is therefore in no simple sense that Hughes wishes to propose our extrication from the consequences that have followed from Man's historical rejection of the Female, as he sees the problem.[125]

Only, the fear in Shakespeare, the pity and the terror, would seem to stem from a deeper source than simply the fear of female sexuality. It is fear of an actual and a complete depravity reigning potentially in us all, to which even woman in her relative innocence is subject. That is the full extent of the Shakespearean despair: all are overwhelmed, and moreover with a violence that does not appear to have limits, except that Shakespeare's characters bear it all in their deaths. From the Shakespearean account, there would seem to be far more in human nature to contend with that would need watching over, some still deeper influence or threat in the blood than what either Graves or Hughes seems ready to acknowledge—some graver menace that Shakespeare would have thought should concern us from our continued embroilment in a fundamental sensuality that defines us all.

Of all the ways in which human nature may be threatened, the experience of subverted love may well be the worst. In Shakespeare the experience is conceived in the absolute terms of our separation from an original, archaic condition of love that has left us utterly vulnerable. Thus Shakespeare could not see any hope *in the immediate term* except directly through our suffering of that separation, or our suffering through it. All the best characters of his imagination are sacrificed to this idea, in the literal sense that all die from it, and that *would* have to drive him further to wonder if this could be all. His coming through beyond this point, as it were back to unity in the Goddess, was as hard a route as any could take, and hardly how we would wish to imagine our way through. Shakespeare's route represents how we would have to come through if we were to act on our hope for ourselves immediately, in our total psychological condition at present, and the cost of that immediate venture is consequently as great as it can be. The tremendously arduous route Shakespeare took from here must for that reason stand *also* in the nature of a warning, as to what we might wish to pretend to from a misplaced idea of our capacities at present.

In comparison with the Shakespearean venture, Graves's venture builds on a peculiar *acceptance* of his immediate condition, and that is Graves's strength. One could hardly deny to him, as we have seen, a profound power to mediate the Goddess's order. He himself involves us in the total reaches of that order, in which the whole range of human experience is accounted for. But it seems that it is enough for him that he has seen that order and that he can fitfully and every so often see it again, and in the meantime is content to think himself very simply into a proper alignment with the Goddess's purposes. This is at the cost, however, of facing more *directly* the greater range of passions with which a man can yet imagine himself contending, it might seem to him hopelessly.[126] Recovering the totality of experience is recognized by Graves as the end goal, but with an *acceptance* of the way things are at present, so long as a proper alignment with this goal is maintained. This perfectly nice, if perfectly profound, adaptation to his situation is what led Hughes to bewail Graves's too strict limitations as a poet, as one critic has pointed out:

> *For all the excitement of the chase, there is something distancing and detached in Graves's evocation of the Goddess. Take, for example, the first line of the dedicatory poem with which the book (**The White Goddess**) opens: "All saints revile her, and all sober men." This is measured, cool, and polished, and virtually lacks any pulse at all. It is as if this control of the verse and the emotion behind it was part of Graves's defense mechanism—a means of controlling the threat of the energy. This may be what Hughes has in mind when he writes of Graves's poetry operating at "some kind of witty, dry distance."*[127]

There is more of careful rationality in Graves than one might have expected of one who was otherwise so critical of Western rationalism. Hughes seems to have felt that *he* took on more, was more aware also (after Reformation man) of his own potential for rejection of the Goddess, was also more aware, as Shakespeare was, that approach to the end-goal would have to involve a greater and more immediate reckoning with those deeper passions that Graves cavalierly puts away. I have quibbled with Hughes, however, for his own relative degree of superficiality, when one refers him to Shakespeare, because Hughes supposes that such passions as a man has to deal with are merely the result of a mistaken perception of the corruption of his beloved or his fear of the Female only.

Any illuminating process which might come to Shakespeare out of humankind's immediate situation, as he understood it, could only come to him by a process of self-growth that few will be able to manage for now. That is because he took *on* more, far more than we are in any position to do ourselves. He was unable to abandon his humankind to their experience, could only see their tragedies through with every one of his ill-fated characters and so, seeing these through, could re-emerge eventually with a far greater perception of the restored mythical totality than even Hughes was able to imagine of him. The corruption by evil is suffered totally, but it is merely suffered; it is not to be understood in terms of any mistaken psychology, hubris, or hamartia, however inevitable, or even as a simple affront to the Goddess. A universal corruption is suffered through totally; it has been the only means for bringing humankind as a whole out of its former condition of sensual embroilment. The consequence of that embroilment has been the extreme violent death of the beloved, marked as this is also by the extreme despair of the hero through whom a prevailing evil has come. The death of Desdemona, the death of Cordelia, as the final consequence of evil: these are challenge enough for now. They are enough of a measure of the tragic tendencies in human nature with which, according to Shakespeare's presentation, we would have to reckon, before we could begin to work our way back into any unity such as would compare with what was formerly ours in the archaic sphere.

Even so, Shakespeare could not *foresee* his re-emergence from tragedy. It was not as if he was conscious of any illuminating power of vision which was his *before* he undertook the plunge into the totality of human errancy. The illuminating process came to him, in fact, from without, from an illuminating power that, at any given moment and at every given stage, remained always fully outside and beyond him, streaming into him and through him strictly from without. He could not have predicted how things would develop, or even that they would. He had been overwhelmed himself, as could only be the case, with the series of deaths that had come from his imagination: Ophelia, Desdemona, Cordelia. From there, for many months it would seem, he lived with the death of the beloved as the symbolic end-consequence of the human tragedy.—Until, with *Pericles*, the light begins, faintly at first, to shine through again, though not without a drastic re-living, a necessary re-surfacing, of the quintessential tragedy—as this takes shape in the death of Thaisa. We have the rest of Shakespeare's progression from here by way of symbolical allegory. At the center of that progression is the experience of the death of the beloved that continually accompanies Shakespeare through the whole series of events that are dramatized right through to the end of *The Tempest*. That death Shakespeare can never leave sight of again, for it represents the outcome of human tragedy itself. Without the continued Imagination of it, there could no longer be for him any further genuine progression. Hence, beyond the death of Thaisa in *Pericles*, there is the death of Hermione in *The Winter's Tale* and the (much overlooked) death of Prospero's wife, each of which symbolizes the fundamental experience of human tragedy Shakespeare could no longer let go of. Out of this *then* comes the further, great experience of the recovery of unity to which Shakespeare's last plays bear witness as a whole. This unity Shakespeare would appear to have been returned to in the most immediate terms only because, having exposed himself fully to the human tragedy, he was now without fear of any further subversion by human nature.

It is a long process, however, by which Shakespeare is brought back to unity. The whole range of tragic experience he had seen through would have to be distributed over all of the last plays in order for that experience to be properly seen and dealt with.[128] That effort involves Shakespeare in a production over years. Thus *Pericles* re-visits the effects of tragedy from the point of view of the hero's fundamental innocence of it; *The Winter's Tale* from the point of view of a complete guiltiness: together they are the combined aspects of Shakespeare's perception of how tragedy has operated in the fates of his tragic characters. Beyond these profound analytical ventures back into the heart of tragic experience, Shakespeare then gives us the fully bodied drama of *The Tempest*. In this play Shakespeare brings the many aspects of the *resolution* of tragedy in turn to bear on the life of Prospero. It is thus Prospero who finally embodies the complete integration in mind and soul that Shakespeare ultimately inherits precisely from the completeness of his progression through tragedy.[129]

One only has to think of what the death of Thaisa in *Pericles*, the death of Hermione in *The Winter's Tale*, and the death of Prospero's wife in *The Tempest* continue to represent symbolically in the way of an experience of human anguish. The experience of human tragedy *continues* in Shakespeare's mind, and when the mythical world finally does break in again on Shakespeare it does so within the terms of this experience. It breaks in on him for the first time when Thaisa recovers, or rather is recovered, from death—*with all that that symbolically implies* of a re-emergence for Shakespeare. In her very first words, as she returns to consciousness, Thaisa calls upon Diana, the Goddess as Virgin, as the ruling Spirit Who underlies this whole action. The Goddess Herself will later appear to Pericles in a dream, to exhort him to make his way to Her temple where Thaisa has lain for as many years as it has taken their lost daughter to come of age. The final reunion of these three in the closing scene of the play represents, in fact, a first significant stage of integration after tragedy for Shakespeare.[130]

The appearance of the Goddess Diana points to a deeper movement of mind and Imagination in Shakespeare that lies well beneath the surface detail. There is an experience of being supported again from being *through* tragedy. That experience is represented as lying at first well outside and beyond where the tragic psyche is at present, as given in the condition of Pericles. The new experience originates in the sphere where Thaisa lies when she is first recovered, well beyond the immediate experience of tragedy through which Pericles continues to live. Fourteen years must go by, a prolonged period of spiritual gestation, before re-integration can begin, during which time the human psyche would seem to be adapting to the tragedy still further, a time in which there is a further, one might say a complete, absorption of the tragedy. Finally the support comes through again. A daughter had sprung in the meantime between the hero and his beloved—a daughter named Marina, and it is she who, having come of age, now appears to Pericles to lift him up again. Who is this daughter but the image of Pericles's own suffering—Shakespeare's own suffering—somehow bearing fruit as a power that now lifts the tragic psyche beyond itself? She is the image of *its* suffering, but now made good:

> she speaks,
> My lord, that, may be, hath endured a grief
> Might equal yours, if both were justly weighed.

How else shall we characterize this daughter but as the enduring self *become* the higher self through which transcendence has come?[131] The tragic psyche or self/Pericles, which in enduring transcends itself, makes itself worthy of uniting with a higher aspect of itself/Marina, and it is this new *integration* in the self that opens the door again to the objective mythical world mediated through Diana. Only *after* this integration in the self does the inspirational dream then come to Pericles that exhorts him to visit Diana's temple, a dream in which Diana Herself appears to him. At this temple he is to rehearse the tragic story that has been his—as if to say that that has been the only way to come to this point and is to continue to be borne in mind. Only thus is Pericles further reunited with his beloved, Thaisa, who is by now a high priestess of Diana—we can only imagine in *what* sphere of higher life together. The reunion takes place in a sphere where the engrossment in sensuality has been virtually abandoned.[132] The process of separation has been drastic and complete. And there is now the return to an experience of mutual support on every hand, with no tragedy subverting: indeed the tragedy has been fully taken up into the new experience.

With *The Winter's Tale* we enter a second stage of re-integration for Shakespeare after tragedy, the *whole* tragedy being re-created again here, through the symbolic death of Hermione, but from the point of view of the tragic hero's complete guiltiness rather than his innocence. A correspondingly deeper suffering is thus enacted in Leontes, which calls for a complete penance, beyond endurance, as befits reckoning with a complete guilt. As in *Pericles*, tragedy is again re-lived but with the birth of a daughter built into it; there is not the death of the beloved alone.

Then follows the same union of the tragic self/Leontes with its higher aspect/Perdita, and from this the still grander re-union with the beloved/Hermione that completes all. Between *Pericles* and *The Winter's Tale*, the self/Shakespeare's own is thus restored from tragedy—by the end of *The Winter's Tale* to a complete integrity again, beyond both innocence and guilt.

As Shakespeare is in progression, more and more of the evolutionary pattern is filled out, with every opportunity given along the way. Thus there is *less* in *The Winter's Tale* of the drama of union between the tragic and higher selves/Leontes and Perdita, because the drama of union in those terms has already been given in *Pericles*. We assume it and fill it out further for ourselves in this second stage. In *The Winter's Tale* the focus is more on the re-union with the beloved/mother/Hermione, which is only imperfectly given in *Pericles*. There is also in *The Winter's Tale* more focus on the relationship to the higher power/Perdita of a *suitor* to that power/Florizel, a relationship that had yet to find any real development in *Pericles* in the relationship between Marina and Lysimachus. A more *direct* relationship is now in development between the daughter and this suitor, which suggests a kind of passing on of the inheritance from the tragic past, as if one might now come into the higher development directly, beyond the error-ridden ways of that past—a form of life projected for the future. But there is the further danger that what is given as an immediate opportunity will itself founder, *without* the connection in consciousness back to the tragic humanity through whose suffering it was brought into being. Hence Camillo's role in this play, who dissuades the young lovers from simply going their own way, directing them back towards Leontes and alerting Polixenes about it so that he follows after them. Camillo in this way brings the young couple back into the circuit of the whole human destiny of which they are the crowning expression or else nothing at all:

> *A course more promising*
> *Than a wild dedication of yourselves*
> *To unpathed waters, undreamed shores, most certain*
> *To miseries enough...*

◆   ◆   ◆

One cannot overstate the achievement that *The Winter's Tale* represents as a perfect harmonizing of the whole tragedy for Shakespeare, one effect of harmonization building successively upon another until we reach the very last scene in which Hermione is restored to Leontes. But the tragedy

The Worst of Depravity 53

is never forgotten, and it is built upon still further in *The Tempest*. Here it appears in the form of the death of Prospero's wife, which is accompanied by the events of treachery that follow upon Prospero's choice of devoting himself to this death. We may imagine Shakespeare in the completeness of his evolution having reached a point where the higher development has grown out still further, as represented in the daughter Miranda, herself a progressive advancement on Perdita—the development, as it were, in yet a third stage. Continuing to read allegorically, the higher self/Miranda is in this case perfectly assimilated by the hero/Prospero, from whom, in spite of the tragedy, she is never separated. The whole inner process has thus been absorbed in Prospero, in whom a certain completeness of development may be assumed. As much is then made of the suitor/Ferdinand's relationship to the daughter/Miranda as in *The Winter's Tale*, and indeed far more, for this now represents Shakespeare's fullest and grandest projection of what our future hope can look like. In this consummate play's dream of a still fuller and fuller harmony spreading over everything, the whole of the outer world is then brought into conjunction with all that is bodied forth in Miranda and Ferdinand as the image of our ideal, restored humanity. Wonder at Miranda is reflected *back* to all, from her who is the very spirit of the *higher* wonder that resides in the mankind she now extols:

> *O brave new world,*
> *That has such people in't!*[133]

Nor has Shakespeare omitted to consider the whole as an *objective* development, ruled over by "the gods" on whom Gonzalo calls to bless this scene: for it is the unitary forces which *they* control that have brought this whole development into being:

> *Look down, you gods,*
> *And on this couple drop a blessed crown!*
> *For it is you that have chalked forth the way*
> *Which brought us hither.*

✦ ✦ ✦

The mythical unity is thus restored in Shakespeare to that point, and on quite another level from when the fierce nature of the primal sensual forces was a part of it. All ferocious sensuality has been removed from the picture that arises out of the world he presents in the end. Here then is another measure of where we stand in relation to the mythical forces about which

Graves has challenged us in modern times. In comparison with Graves Shakespeare offers a more complete picture of what we can understand to be at stake. From Shakespeare's point of view, there would appear to be far more of human nature to contend with, far more of a struggle with this nature to anticipate, and consequently more of a prospect following from our ultimate success with this struggle. It is a view that looks more boldly to the future on the basis of a far more courageous consideration of our whole nature as inherited from our archaic past. Contrastingly, Graves's view is of our situation in relation to the basic prospect, looking out from a standpoint somewhere between before and after, as it were out of our *present* embroilment in our sensual nature, to the limited extent that we may speak of our coming to terms with it.

We will now consider yet another approach to the mythical forces—in the case of Keats, whom I have chosen as a kind of spokesman for another range of effort. *His* effort lies somewhere in between Shakespeare's involvement in all that is inwardly at stake in relation to those forces, and Graves's more fitful Imaginative engagement, which, if psychologically reckless, yet took him to the brink of an objective image-making, or pictoriality, that would also appear to be intrinsic to the mythical experience. Looking at Keats will allow us to see also where the *Romantic* sensibility might be said to lie in relation to this experience. And so with that we shall have covered still more of the range of the *historical* effort that has engaged Western man in his desire to think himself again into the fullness of the world in which the Goddess, it has been thought, continues to rule.

III
IMPASSE OF THE IMAGINATION

I

It is well-known that Keats envisioned his *own* connection back into the Goddess's order and to the fullness of the mythical creation with which She is directly associated also by him. The prospect of an ultimate union with the Goddess is allegorically projected in "Endymion"; an eventual "happiness" is conceived in these terms. But Endymion must live, for now, through the tragic frustration of separation from his Beloved. He lives in a form of dispossession the inverse of that experienced by Venus with Adonis in their classic story. There are, however, many intimations of the final union with his Goddess that is to come. He is already endowed by Her with the power to penetrate the underworld. Here he attends directly on Adonis's blissful re-awakening to Venus after his usual winter's sleep. Venus Herself inspires Endymion to hope, by foretelling his own reunion with his beloved Goddess. And so he continues to think happiness in spite of being returned at this moment to his solitary self, cut off once again in his earthly condition from the super-earthly vision with which he has momentarily been blessed.

Endymion witnessing the moment of Adonis's revival prefigures the power over death that Keats could project for himself from an Imaginative connection to *his* Goddess. The vision of that power is extended in the later episode with Glaucus. Here Endymion assumes a role of savior for *all* lovers who have been severed by tragic fortune in a world hostile to their union. Soon his heart is itself captured by an Indian maid of flesh and blood, but he feels he has, in this merely temporal love, in the meantime compromised his passion for his Goddess. He is thrown into a state of utter lassitude and dejected resignation from his now conflicted condition.[134] In the Cave of Quietude that he then reaches, all speaks to him of his readiness to abide in the mystery of his own uncertainty, removed at once from his ideal goal and his earthly object. It is not hard to see in this situation an anticipation of the more highly evolved rendering, in the "Ode to a Nightingale", of that same suspended open-ness to fate that we associate with Keats's idea of "negative capability". The episode in the Cave has been seen as the problematic climax to "Endymion" and its *actual* end, in contrast with the poem's formal ending, which seems to *force* a union between the ideal and the earthly, simply to complete the pattern predicted for its action.

Somewhere over the course of revising "Endymion", it would appear that Keats conceived of a new major poem, the epic "Hyperion".[135] With this poem Keats stepped still *further* back into the archaic world he had already been presenting, taking himself back to the time when Saturn and his fellow Titans had just been dethroned, by the lesser gods of Olympus. However, this focus marks a significant alteration in Keats's approach, for he had now conceived the idea of an *evolution* through worlds. Evolution, in some form or other, had come *from* the separation from the archaic unity—tragic though that separation is also. Apollo, as the god who is to supercede Hyperion—the last of the older gods from Saturn's reign to retain power—points to the possibility of a fuller experience of the world *in knowledge*. Keats is clearly suspended now between his primal commitment to the archaic unity, which the former reign of Saturn represents, and his understanding that the experience of the world that has been had since will also have to receive his commitment. Apollo cannot rest until he has known all about the world he is helping to bring into being. Through this focus on the moment of Apollo's instalment, Keats is allegorically envisaging the possibility also of exploring his own state of knowledge as a poet in his present condition, separated from, yet continuing in a relationship to, the archaic unity.

But the thought of where he stood with his own present condition would appear to have driven Keats, in a further development, to consider his older epic approach to his theme outmoded, so that he soon felt forced to abandon the "Hyperion". Not long before he undertook the writing of "Hyperion" Keats had met Fanny Brawne. The meeting inspired him to take up the poetic cause he had set for himself with a renewed sense of all that he felt he could accomplish. But then the realization set in that he had more to make of his own experience in the present, and "Hyperion" was abandoned. That understanding coincided with a development in passion in his relationship to Fanny. In "The Eve of St. Agnes" Keats's ideal ambitions now give way to a forthright affirmation of the predominant value of his earthly love for Fanny. In the poem, Porphyry, the male lover, is intent on persuading his beloved Madeline to accept that, steeped as they may be in an ideal dream of love, it is finally the *reality* of love that matters. What matters is that they have each other now, in flesh and blood. And Keats's characters *will* escape in the dead of night, defying all conventions, into a new world that is now theirs in reality, if still hedged round with the deep mystery of love. So Porphyry and Madeline disappear together at the end into the storm that bears at least some marks of the world of archaic mystery of that poem.

The turning point in the poem is when Porphyry succeeds in rousing Madeline from her visionary dream of the love of him (brought on by a potion she has taken) by singing into her ears the story of "La Belle Dame Sans Merci". The singing of that song seems to be intended (by Porphyry) to suggest that there is something of the unreal cruelty of that Dame in Madeline while she continues to lie in a mere swoon of love, more content with the idea of it than the reality. However that may be, within a few months Keats had indeed written his famous poem on that subject, as if he had been made aware, in the meantime, of a power in Fanny to dispossess him of any hope of love in the real world. She had reverted in this poem to being the cruel and elusive Dame, possessed of an otherworldly power of love that could only leave Keats, as her lover and knight errant, at the complete mercy of her influence over him. The two poles of earthly and ideal destiny are thus brought again into seemingly impossible opposition to each other. Here was the very situation in real terms that Keats had allegorically prophesized for himself in "Endymion". Only, the opposition had polarized even further.

In "La Belle Dame" one might think Keats had found his way directly to the Goddess on whom he had attended since "Endymion". "La Belle Dame" Graves saw as one of the central expressions of the Goddess's influence in English poetry.[136] But in this poem the Goddess appears as the *counterpole* to the all-harmonizing entity Keats had made of her in "Endymion". She *was* that entity until the tension between earthly and ideal commitments drives Endymion into that intense area of uncertainty that would only seem to make him ready to accept any outcome. Keats would appear to have entered in this later period, between "St. Agnes" and "La Belle Dame", into roughly the same condition Endymion is in when worn out by his own impasse. That Keats could not rest content with a relationship to the Goddess such as he presents in "La Belle Dame" is a significant measure of his complex distance from Graves's own indulgent aesthetic about Her—Keats demanding more, by way of a total satisfaction.

The further transformation Keats undergoes at this point is extraordinary, for it suddenly points a direction the *opposite* of that on which he seemed bent until now in referring himself to the archaic unity. His case represents, in fact, the complete counterpole to the concern with the mythical-archaic that has occupied *us* thus far. Keats would appear in this period to have found himself acting on the idea of the necessity of a *modern* production opposed to the archaic: a new project that he had been turning over in his mind for over a year. It appears that he saw in

Wordsworth his model in this direction: his model in renunciation. In the previous April he had turned

> to the large question...whether Wordsworth has indeed a potential epic sweep, and has thus "martyred himself to the human heart"—martyred the freer, older uses of poetry to the inevitably pressing needs of the modern age.[137]

Keats's original ambition, in conceiving of "Hyperion", had been to set his account of the evolution of consciousness into the greater framework of archaic origins and ultimate ends, and so his idea of a major poem that might rival any of the ancients (from the Greeks to Milton):

> a poem in which, however much he would try to follow out what he felt to be the great modern challenge to poetry, he also naturally wanted to catch what he could of the amplitude and vigor that we honor in earlier works while fearing to do other than imitate our contemporaries.[138]

> Apollo's painful evolution into growing consciousness would tap, perhaps closely parallel, personal experiences of his own.[139]

But, as we have seen, knowledge would mean, sooner than Keats had planned, knowledge of his own condition in the present, especially as

> now Keats began to think of history as a process in which the changes that take place are fundamental. Men and their achievements must be seen in relation to the age in which they live.[140]

However, Keats had not anticipated being plunged into a new mode of poetic uncertainty, at the opposite end from that older mode in which the results had seemed foretold:

> the situation would involve an additional loneliness that he had not anticipated, and it certainly emphasized the distance still to be travelled.[141]

> With every further step in knowledge, to be sure, the

inscrutable mystery of things seems only to deepen, and the uncertainty of human judgements to become more obvious.[142]

But

In this protective labyrinth, still to be explored, there will be a "sanctuary" with all that a "working brain" may find or construct

Naturally there will be uncertainty...there is the possibility of mere illusion as well as creativity.

thought will inevitably be "shadowy"...[143]

Yet if, at the moment, "We see not the balance..." and "are in a mist," that only means that the life of thinking man must be a search...[144]

The immediate first result of this new poetic life, on which Keats embarked at this time was the "Ode to Psyche". On first appearance this poem will strike us as a simple carry-over from the archaic mode of Keats's mythic ambitions. There is the direct apostrophe to the Goddess in the poem's first line, as if Keats might be settled elsewhere than in his modern present, and there is also the poem's basic fictional drama, which sets us in the immediate company of Cupid and his beloved Psyche. Do we assume that Keats projects himself in their company as they were of old? Or are we not more likely to see this as, quite self-consciously, fiction? Yet Keats in this poem is claiming 'actually' to see them immediately in his Imagination in the present moment. It is his boast that *he* is the one, in this late age, to have discovered Psyche as the "latest born and loveliest far/Of all Olympus's faded hierarchy", whom no ancient religion had ever formally recognized.[145] And he is now to be Her priest and poet.

It is true that Keats laments that there can be no form of religious expression in his day to compare with the way his discovered Goddess would have been honored in the past, had She been known then. This also suggests a throwback to the archaic setting in which Keats's Imagination had been immersed to this point. Some consciousness remains of his tragic distance from the full-fledged directness with which he imagines the transcendent realities of Nature to have been celebrated then. But he feels the momentousness of his own role as priest to his Goddess all the more, precisely from knowing that a new venture must consequently arise out of the present, and it is *as a comparative metaphor* that Keats is here drawing on the effective power projected of archaic religious practice. That the archaic detail has turned into comparative metaphor we might have deduced from the explicit subject of Keats's poem—Psyche, that is the Mind itself, and so by deduction his own mind in relation to that greater Mind's Imaginative promptings *as these can be known in the present*. His own mind, or Imagination, had now become the object of Keats's devotion, to draw on at will for the further exploration of reality, which might now take almost any direction. That his focus has turned inward is made explicit in the poem's last stanza, where the poet speaks of building a temple

> *In some untrodden region of my mind,*
> *Where branched thoughts, new grown with pleasant pain,*
> *Instead of pines shall murmur in the wind:*

It is also significant that Keats should *continue* with the natural imagery from this point, which has now converted into metaphors for the Mind's own experience, its own infinite depths of subtle variety and invention:

> *Far, far around shall those dark-clustered trees*
> *Fledge the wild-ridged mountains steep by steep;*
> *And there by zephyrs, streams, and birds, and bees,*
> *The moss-lain Dryads shall be lull'd to sleep;*

With the reference to Dryads here, some part of the archaic world has been internalized, but in this new sanctuary of his own mind, the Imagination, combining Mind with Love (Cupid), will be free to search out and to create at will, to forecast and to conclude as *it* deems right. Here Keats had reached the point he had projected for himself when a year earlier he had spoken of "the Chamber of Maiden Thought" into which one comes out of a first "infant or thoughtless Chamber"—this last being the Chamber he had been in while given to his automatic allegiance to the epic-archaic ideal he had derived from Milton. Beyond the second Chamber, of Maiden Thought, lies still *another* that Keats was now poised to enter:

> *Well—I compare human life to a large Mansion of Many*
> *apartments, two of which I can only describe, the doors of*
> *the rest being as yet shut upon me—The first we step into*

> *we call the infant or thoughtless Chamber, in which we remain as long as we do not think—We remain there a long while, and notwithstanding the doors of the second Chamber remain wide open, showing a bright appearance, we care not to hasten to it; but are at length imperceptibly impelled by the awakening of the thinking principle within us—we no sooner get into the second Chamber, which I shall call the Chamber of Maiden-Thought, than we become intoxicated with the light and the atmosphere, we see nothing but pleasant wonders, and think of delaying there forever in delight. However, among the effects this breathing is father of is that tremendous one of sharpening one's vision into the heart and the nature of Man—of convincing one's nerves that the world is full of Misery and Heartbreak, Pain, Sickness and Oppression—whereby this Chamber of Maiden Thought becomes gradually darken'd and at the same time on all sides of it many doors are set open—but all dark—all leading to dark passages—We see not the balance of good and evil. We are in a Mist—We are now in that state—We feel the "burden of the Mystery,"*[146]

Keats had for the first time reached this third Chamber, which he leaves unnamed, with his "Ode to a Nightingale" and his "Ode on a Grecian Urn". With the illuminating consciousness he had broken into, as the "Ode to Psyche" presents this, identical with his inward-turning Imagination, Keats was now set to take on whatever of human suffering he could manage to draw within the scope of that Imagination.[147] This Imagination is *immediately* conceived in relation to human suffering, and human suffering to the Imagination, so that in "Nightingale" Keats can *begin* in the very midst of this suffering:

> *My heart aches, and a drowsy numbness pains my sense…*

From this suffering, however, Keats is drawn up into his Imagination as the immediate counterbalance to it, although no sooner has he found wings for flight than he is brought back, in another remarkable inversion, to the seemingly irrepressible condition of suffering—

> *Where but to think is to be full of sorrow*
> *And leaden-eyed despairs*

A significant distinction is thus drawn between the terrible human suffering that is our lot, and the beautiful ideal, at the other extreme, of the aspiring Imagination, which the world of our suffering is bound to wear away at:

> *Where Beauty cannot keep her lustrous eyes*
> *Or new Love pine at them beyond to-morrow.*

Characteristic of his situation now, the opposition of suffering only drives Keats to seek *more* of the Imagination, to penetrate more deeply into it:

> *Away, away! For I will fly to thee*

it might seem only in order to escape from his suffering, except that his suffering remains bound up with his Imagination. It is more to the point that in penetrating more deeply into the world of Imagination Keats comes more fully into a power that *transmutes* his suffering, or that at least affirms the ideal ever more strongly against it. It is a world that offers an inexhaustible potential for re-orientation and renewal, immediately supported as Keats is in the tenderness and in the complete richness of the Imagination's influence, which incorporates only the beautiful in Nature and the terrible into the beautiful. That we have here entered a purely inward world is broadcast to us in the language distinctive of Keats's effort in this stage:

> *But here there is no light*
> *Save what from heaven is with the breezes blown*
> *Through verdurous glooms and winding mossy ways.*

> *I cannot see...*
> ....

> *But, in embalmed darkness, guess each sweet...*

Keats gives himself to his Imagination, in fact, as his own voice, which is now creating *out* of the world that he has penetrated, taking us up along with him. He is inspired by the *supreme* voice of the Nightingale, which, out of this world, apotheosizes the Imaginative power in its seemingly infinite resourcefulness. In a further supreme twist, this seems to Keats then the finest moment in which to die, while he is utterly given to the beauty-making power of his Imagination, which can make a beautiful thing also of the moment of death:

> *Now more than ever seems it rich to die,*
> *To cease upon the midnight with no pain,*
> *While thou art pouring forth thy soul abroad*
> *In such an ecstasy!*

But this triumphant moment immediately prompts the further thought that in the meantime *he* will have turned to dust,

> *Still wouldst thou sing, and I have ears in vain—*
> *To thy high requiem become a sod.*

The Imaginative power, for its part, will have remained behind and beyond him, intact as it always has been through the generations. That he has now become concerned with what becomes of us individually does not stop him from speculating more about the Imagination itself, and he is finally left wondering how real his life is in comparison with *its* reality. But even so his concern has *become* the individual death—his own death, as an instance of the death of each one of us. And it could only have been a natural thing for him to proceed from here to the "Grecian Urn" as his next object of focus.

The title of this poem, "Ode on a Grecian Urn", immediately sets us in relation to death, and to the ashes that this urn contained, or was meant to contain, at one time. We imagine the owner commissioning the sculpting of an elaborate scene onto the urn intended *for* him, or perhaps sculpting it onto this urn himself. Set all around its solid frame is a scene depicting the effects of human passion as at some ancient orgiastic religious festival. Men in this scene merge with gods, in pursuit of maidens who are loath to be caught but are otherwise themselves caught up in the "wild ecstasy" of this celebration. At this scene there is also a playing of pipes and of timbrels, and soon the poet has immersed himself in the action, conscious of the fact that it captures an effect of life lived in the moment of the happiest passion, preserved in this artistic expression as if forever. Trees and their boughs, the piper himself, as the "happy melodist" of the poem, piping his song, the lovers in pursuit of each other—all have remained as they are, intact from the ravages of time, preserved in this moment of the happiest passion. The best of human life has in this way been saved from death, the Imagination of the sculptor having exercised itself in a supreme temporal expression of its power. No greater possibility could be conceived.

Like Keats, applying himself in his own Imaginative power to this scene[148], the sculptor/owner has brought his Imagination to bear to the fullest possible extent on the physical fact of death as represented by the ashes in the urn. How sublime the effect when we imagine Keats imagining his own ashes in that urn! Clearly he had brought his idea of the opposing claims of death and of the Imagination into the greatest possible tension here. The terrible effects of passion over time—

> *That leaves a heart high-sorrowful and cloy'd*
> *A burning forehead and a parching tongue.*

are in this scene pre-empted as if forever. But in the meantime our attention is brought back to the actuality of the desolation that lies everywhere beyond the scene depicted on the urn. There is the account of the also forever silent streets that have been emptied of the folk that have flocked to this triumphant festival:

> *And, little town, thy streets for evermore*
> *Will silent be; and not a soul to tell*
> *Why thou art desolate, can e'er return.*

The frame of reference extends here surely also to us as *we* gather around Keats while reading this poem.

We have thus in the end been merely "*teased* out of [the] thought" of death, though we are left possessed at the same time of perhaps the finest form of consolatory expression art can devise, within the scope of the possibilities available to the Imagination. This becomes our way of understanding what the urn is finally said to proclaim out of itself:

> "*Beauty is truth, truth beauty, that is all*
> *Ye know on earth, and all ye need to know.*"

Art, by its power to absorb us totally *in* the beautiful, beyond the terrible reality of our mortality, expresses all that it is possible to express of the truth of the Imagination. Beyond that expression, however, lies another truth—the truth of the desolation of reality of which we are a part when we are returned to dust. But it has sufficed in the meantime that we are and will have been consoled while we are alive, and for that the Imagination is there—for that art has been there.

It is, however, as far as Keats could go with the beauty-making power of his Imagination. He had far more to say *about* it in his illustrious Letters. He had been, for over a year, through an intense if quiet period of preparation, and it is clear that he had then profited immensely from the inspiration of Fanny's immediate presence in the house which he now shared with her along with her mother and his friend Brown. But Brown's house would have to be rented for the summer, and the separation from Fanny that ensued would cut him off from his inspiration. He had in any case reached with "Urn" an extraordinary end-point beyond which he could not go and could never have gone. He had taken the claims of the Imagination, upon which he had alighted so momentously, as far as they *could* go. And how, one might ask, could he not then do as he did do, which is return to the old production with which he had long been identified, before his sudden plunge into his modern present?

Thus followed "Lamia" and a return to "Hyperion", which had now become "The Fall of Hyperion", in both of which we may divine a new despair and a more serious falling away from himself. His perception of the influences of love had taken a still more drastic turn (from "La Belle Dame") in "Lamia". Suddenly the beloved has become, at the other extreme from La Dame, a figure of hopeless demonic import (in opposition to the figure of hopeless heavenly import of La Dame)—embodying Keats's condition of frustrated passion at this time.[149] The final formal judgment of Lamia in the poem expresses no settled position in Keats but is itself part of the hopeless dialectic of Keats's problem in his frustration.[150] As for "The Fall", this poem Keats would eventually, as in the case of its earlier version as "Hyperion", likewise abandon. He was all the more likely to abandon it after the Odes, which makes Keats's choice of returning to this subject seem like a desperate one. His immersion in his own modern present, complete as this had been, and indeed extreme, would have dispossessed him of any connection back to this outworn form of production. And yet it is clear that the idea of the epic-archaic project had not left Keats. Indeed, how could it, seeing as this was, for him also, and would have to be, the primordial concern of the poetic-Imaginative life in one form or another?

In one respect at least "The Fall" represents a kind of advancement on the "Urn"—in the case of the so-called "Induction" to the poem, which represents a new stage of vision for Keats. But it is still so much in an earlier outworn mode (for all its remarkable graces, derived from Dante) that surely Keats could see there was no future in it for him. In content, if not in form, it represents an advancement.[151] After envisioning his own death in "Urn", and surviving the deprivations that had come from separation from Fanny, it is easy to conceive Keats in the condition that is noted of the poet in the "Induction":

> *Thou hast felt*
> *What 'tis to die and live again before*
> *Thy fated hour*

The poet is suddenly projected into the typical world of the medieval dream-vision, but before he comes into his vision of Moneta, he pledges himself to

> *all the mortals of the world,*
> *And all the dead whose names are on our lips,*

The phrasing is a throwback to the episode in "Endymion" when Keats saw himself as the savior of all lovers who had died separated from each other. It appeared now as if he had indeed come to the verge of that role in his life. The air that greets him in this new world of vision is said to be filled

> *with so much pleasant health*
> *That even the dying man forgets his shroud*

Keats, it would appear, could now think himself into a still further sphere in which, like Shakespeare, the world's tragedies can no longer leave him, a sphere in which he can only occupy himself with these tragedies, and it is precisely this choice of life that has won him his unique audience with the envisioned Moneta. But this apparent advance in vision can only lead Keats back to his epic-archaic project, specifically to "Hyperion" (now re-named "The Fall"). And so this Moneta Keats presents predictably as the last surviving Power out of the Golden Age over which Saturn formerly ruled before this world was overturned by the Olympians. It is She who since that time has been

> *left supreme,*
> *Sole priestess of this desolation*

And the poet is the one who, by his extreme commitment to human suffering has worked his way to Her (he is valued less as a poet than as a dreamer or visionary of this kind). Scenes of that "high tragedy" are now to unfold in vision before the poet out of Moneta's "globed brain" where they lie stored up in memory.

It is not difficult to see that Keats had always had the idea of epically referring the particulars of human destiny back to a primordial unitary life which he associates with the reign of Saturn before his Fall. Human suffering was for him an expression of that Fall, and Keats could feel that, in the completeness of his own commitment to human suffering, he had reached the stage of identifying himself with that Fall. One can only imagine what he would have wished to do from here. One could see him pursuing the tragedy farther along in time, at least (for now) to the point of the Fall of Hyperion, the last God from that earlier Age to give up his primal power. Apollo was to be his successor, he Whom Keats in the earlier "Hyperion" had addressed as "the Father of all verse." A first stage in the evolutionary development of the world would have thus been reached. It would be the poet's role to transmute suffering, but there was now the role, beyond the poet, of the dreamer or visionary, who in a further development can bring humankind back to the primal unity, beyond suffering and death, an act that would correspond to a restoration of Saturn's former reign.

This was quite the epic project, but only the kind of thing the poets of the Romantic Age, to which Keats belonged, imagined for themselves as the end-goal of their visionary-poetic striving.[152] But as a *form*, or mode of production, the older style could hardly have done the job any longer of convincingly embodying the quality of human suffering and of human expression of Keats's own time. The already prescribed externality of the older style could never have left room for an appropriate expression of present inner development. And yet, how far could the plunge towards modernity, into the strictly present moment of the Imagination, have taken Keats? Having confined himself so strictly to the present moment, he had gone with the Imagination as far as it could go, for the pure inwardness of *this* mode could never have converted into any further external development. It leaves him in the end with no further possible power over his destiny than what he depicts in "Urn".

He had, it is true, made a further advance in experience, as expressed in the Induction to "The Fall", but as we have seen is immediately claimed again by the outworn style. That it was an advance in experience from the point he had reached in "Urn", and as such extraordinary, who can doubt, but one can only feel that Keats would have done better to begin with a completely new poem, and with a more direct approach, perhaps along the lines of the one Coleridge had made in "Kubla Khan".[153] If we are to believe

Middleton Murry, it would appear that Keats *misconceived* of his role as an epic poet, in the comparison with Wordsworth. Wordsworth never had given himself to the modern at the expense of the "older uses of poetry":

> *Wordsworth is not claiming*[154] *that he has 'epic passion' and that he 'martyrs this to the human heart'; but that his poem is to be more than the equivalent of Milton's epic, and is (so to speak) to be the veritable epic of the human soul.*[155]

> *If Milton's work were to be emulated, it could only be emulated as Wordsworth emulated it, by attempting to create an epic of the rediscovery of vital religion in the experience of prophetic man.*[156]

There could only have been for Wordsworth a form of epic poetry that arose "prophetically", that is to say anterior to outer forms, from the human soul itself, for which Keats in his own way might have been eminently suitable if he had not been from early on so obsessed by those "older uses" of poetry to which he had adhered, following Milton. In the reactionary turn towards the modern, Keats had then *also* gone too far. With him the human soul then became its own end, to the point where he stood without any further relation to an objective otherworld that might counterbalance it from the other side. Keats had thus *generally* reached impasse, in relation to which he does not appear to have made any further headway. And it will seem fitting, if sad, that his last great poem should be his "Ode To Autumn". Keats had inevitably turned his attention back to the scene of outer nature, on all that stands in full harvest but is also at the point of death, which is just where Keats found himself, before the final decline.

Some external inward would have to be grabbed hold of once again, if the mythic unity *were* to be recovered, and this the Romantic Imagination, for all the extension of experience one finds in it, was finally unable to do. The Romantics found themselves caught between the old and the new, and in Keats's case it finally led to too much of the new: to an *over*-valuation of the human soul, at the expense of any further relation to an objective otherworld. One would be able to cite innumerable critics and readers who have over the years made an ideal of the modern scepticism of Keats: his ultimate regard for the earthly above the ethereal or the super-earthly, the natural above the visionary etc.[157] But that way of appreciating Keats has really been our own modern way; it has expressed our own fundamental bias, for it overlooks the fact that Keats found himself, as a result of his going in that direction, ultimately alienated from the mythical destiny that, like all of his fellow Romantics, still concerned him very much.

At the same time, as we have seen, an archaic style out of the past had *over*claimed his attention, with the result that he had dispossessed himself of any authentic relation to the mythical sphere from that side also. He was more aware of being mistaken in this respect than were Shelley or Byron, for example.[158] Graves's efforts to re-connect with the mythical, though they may seem to revert to something much older[159], in fact make the very old new again. In contrast with the Romantics, however, no account of a process of inner growth, in his case, testifies to the path that led him to his amazing breakthrough. Graves had claimed, in fact, some form of *immediate* transposition of the poet into the frenzied visionary condition that allows him to re-connect again. The poet was, indeed, for him,

> *a deutero-potmos: a second-fated one who has, as it were,* **already** *died, and conversed with the oracular dead*[160]

Perhaps in this context we should not be making light of the fact that Graves *had* passed through a form of death, literally on the battlefield, and had in fact at one point been declared dead.

Death will surely come into it at some point. Shakespeare had had the relative leisure to imagine himself, over many years, into the suffering and death of his characters, and thereby *drove* himself into a new mythical world. Keats, with the Odes, stands in his newly conceived power of Imagination, as we have seen, over and against death, which *he* brings into focus as our final destiny impervious to all further scrutiny. He was then cut off from further production when his fatal illness set in, not long after the period we have covered. He had, just before that, progressed to a state in which it seemed to him he literally knew what it was like " to die, and live again before/ [His] fated hour." He was now living with death in a new way, and from this condition came his extraordinary imagination of Moneta, which *might* have issued out into a new relation to the mythical.[161] For any one of various reasons that prospect was not to be, but I have noted how along the way Keats had seriously bipolarized himself, separating himself radically from the mythical quest by indulging in our own modern bias of immersion in the strictly present moment of the Imagination. When, inevitably, he came back to the mythical quest, he had no more developed a form of his own for coming to terms with that quest than when he had opted to retreat from it—ending up as sadly baffled as when he had left off...

Endnotes

1. A matter that I began to address myself with my chapter on Sylvia Plath in *The Modern Debacle*, New York: IUniverse, 2007.
2. See Appendix B in *The White Goddess*, ed., Grevel Lindop, London: Faber, 1999, 489-504.
3. The review is directly brought up in Graves's lecture. It first appeared in *The Yale Review* in the 1956 Winter and Spring issues, and was later collected in Randall Jarrell's *The Third Book of Criticism*, Farrar, Straus & Giroux, 1965, 75-112.
4. *The Third Book*, 112.
5. *The Third Book*, 90.
6. *The White Goddess*, 13.
7. All references to *The Complete Poems*, ed., Dunstan Ward and Beryl Graves, London: Penguin, 2003.
8. See, for example, Mircea Eliade who speaks (in connection with another kind of initiation having to do with a return to the womb) of "the adventures of Heroes or of shamans and magicians...in their flesh-and-blood bodies, not symbolically." *Myth and Reality*, New York: Harper and Row, 1963, 81.
9. The further question will be raised, of course, how *woman* undergoes this grandiose destiny. As we shall see, as the one in whom the Goddess directly reflects something of Herself, the Goddess being up to a point in fact "incarnate in every woman", woman must necessarily experience the whole cycle of death and rebirth in her own way, though this matter is not gone into anywhere in Graves, as far as I know. As a male poet, clearly Graves narrates his "story" largely from his male perspective, although given his orientation towards the Goddess,

he is necessarily involved in offering some highly subtle views of woman's own role and experience in this picture. For a more complete picture of these views than can be offered here, see my chapter on Graves in my book, *The Modern Debacle*.
10. *The White Goddess*, 20.
11. As in the Indian mythology, for one. See, for example, the illustration provided by Joseph Campbell in his *Hero With a Thousand Faces*, Princeton: Princeton Univ. Press, 1973; orig. pub., 1949, between 228 and 229. Italian Renaissance art, drawing directly on ancient Roman models, bears further, abundant testimony to this graphic mythical subject. See Edith Balas, *The Mother Goddess in Italian Renaissance Art*, Pittsburgh: Carnegie Mellon University Press, 2002, 6 and 120 *passim*. **The lion**, as a constant attribute of the Goddess, represented, generally, the savagery of the earth and the wildness of the brute—in Graves's own terms human beastliness as well: all tamed by, or brought under the controlling power of, the Goddess originally (see Balas, 22-23 and 59n.26.) However, at a certain point, as we shall see when we turn to Shakespeare, humankind becomes fully responsible for itself, which is the occasion of great despair in the first place.
12. Terms that draw on Graves's idea of the effectiveness of what he calls a "true" poem, in *The White Goddess*, 20: "The reason why the hairs stand on end, the eyes water, the throat is constricted, the skin crawls and a shiver runs down the spine when one writes or reads a true poem is that a true poem is necessarily an invocation of the White Goddess…"
13. Readers who wish to follow the complex, evolving fortunes of the poet and his beloved, beyond what is only hinted at in this study, should be referred to my chapter on Graves in *The Modern Debacle*. See also below for Keats's own presentation of an evolving relationship between poet and his beloved.
14. See Ivan Stenski, *Four Theories of Myth in Twentieth Century History*, Bassingstoke, Macmillan, 1987, 75.
15. *Myth and Reality*, 139.
16. *Myth and Reality*, 142.
17. *Myth and Reality*, 141.
18. *Myth and Reality*, 12.
19. *Myth and Reality*, 141.
20. See my study, *The Modern Debacle*.
21. *Myth and Reality*, 192-193.

22. Stenski, 128.
23. Stenski, 128.
24. *Myth and Reality*, 190: "Everything leads us to believe that the reduction of "artistic universes" to the primordial state of *materia prima* is only a phase in a more complex process, just as, in the cyclic conceptions of the archaic and traditional societies, "Chaos", the regression of all forms to the indistinction of the *materia prima*, is followed by a new Creation, which can be homologized with a cosmogony."
25. Stenski, 102. Nostalgia, incidentally, was an intrinsic feature of Camus's philosophy, as in *The Myth of Sisyphus*.
26. *Myth and Reality*, 192.
27. *Myth and Reality*, 189.
28. *Myth and Reality*, 188.
29. Ernst Cassirer, *Language and Myth*, New York: Dover, 1953, 94.
30. *Language and Myth*, 99.
31. *Language and Myth*, 99.
32. *Language and Myth*, 99.
33. *Language and Myth*, 99.
34. *Language and Myth*, 37.
35. *Language and Myth*, 62.
36. Cassirer (*Language and Myth*, 45) expands upon this matter as follows: "some indirect relationship must obtain, which covers everything from the most primitive gropings of mythico-religious thought to those highest products in which such thought seems to have already gone over into a realm of pure speculation."
37. Among these one might put together the following synopsis: "Mythical thinking…is captivated and enthralled by the intuition which suddenly confronts it. The ego is spending all its energy on this single object, lives in it, loses itself in it. Only when this intense individuation has been consummated, when the immediate intuition has been focused and, one might say, reduced to a single point, does the mythic or linguistic form emerge, and the word or the momentary god is created. At this point, the word which denotes that thought content is not a mere conventional symbol, but is merged with its object in an indissoluble unity. What significance the part in question may have in the structure and coherence of the whole, what function it fulfils, is relatively unimportant—the mere fact that it is or has been a part, that it has been connected with the whole, no matter

how casually, is enough to lend it the full significance and power of that greater unity. Whoever has brought any part of a whole into his power has thereby acquired power, in the magical sense, over the whole itself." (*Language and Myth*, 32, 57, 58, 92.) That "whole", that "greater unity", Graves might be thought to have himself brought forward in that great centre-piece of his poetic oeuvre, "To Juan at the Winter Solstice".

38. Owen Barfield, *Poetic Diction*, London: Faber, 1962, 86.
39. *Poetic Diction*, 92.
40. *Poetic Diction*, 85.
41. *Poetic Diction*, 34.
42. *Poetic Diction*, 32.
43. Owen Barfield, *Saving the Appearances*, London: Faber, 1957, 142.
44. *Poetic Diction*, 32.
45. *Poetic Diction*, 32. Durkheim is quoted from *The Elementary Forms of the Religious Life*.
46. *Saving the Appearances*, 126. In my section on Barfield I am, of course, bound to reproduce his own homocentric terms, although it is clear that while "man" or "archaic man", as terms, will be accepted of a cultural past largely fashioned by men, they are hardly suitable for a future in which women, no doubt from quite another perspective, will also be doing much of that cultural-artistic fashioning or "creation" Barfield anticipates happening. I have myself offered a brief treatment of Sylvia Plath's unique production from this point of view, in *The Modern Debacle*.
47. *Appearances*, 142.
48. *Appearances*, 144.
49. *Appearances*, 144.
50. *Appearances*, 127.
51. *Appearances*, 127.
52. *Appearances*, 131-132.
53. *Appearances*, 144.
54. *Appearances*, 121.
55. See *Symbols of Transformation*, New York: Harper, 1962, 224.
56. "Graves and the White Goddess" from *The Third Book of Criticism*, 107.
57. *Symbols of Transformation*, 232.
58. *Symbols*, 232.
59. *Symbols*, 227.
60. *Symbols*, 227.

61. *Symbols*, 232.
62. *Hero With a Thousand Faces*, 10. Clearly the male point of view on this issue is assumed by Campbell here, as indeed also by Jung in the section of *his* work I have quoted.
63. Cf. *The White Goddess*, 334: "an obvious difference between poems and dreams is that in poems one is (or should be) in critical control of the situation; in dreams one is a paranoiac, a mere spectator of the mythographic event".
64. *Hero*, 256-257.
65. *Hero*, 257.
66. *Hero*, 118.
67. *Hero*, 114.
68. *Hero*, 137.
69. Cf. Barfield on Jung: "the traditional myths and the archetypes which he tells us are the representations of the collective unconscious, are assumed by him to be, and always to have been, neatly insulated from the world of nature with which , according to their own account, they were mingled or united... The psychological interpretation of mythology...when it actually comes up against the nature-content of the myths...still relies on the old anthropological assumption of 'projection.' (*Appearances*, 134-135)
70. *Hero*,115.
71. In "Conjunction", for example, Graves intuits the final unity for himself.
72. *The White Goddess*, 476. Campbell himself assumes the possibility of progression, but could allow for much relativity along the way: "As [a man] progresses in the slow initiation which is life, the form of the goddess undergoes for him a series of transfigurations: she can never be greater than himself, though she can always promise him more than he is yet capable of comprehending. She lures, she guides, she bids him burst his fetters. And if he can match her import, the two, the knower and the known, will be released from every limitation. Woman is the guide to the sublime acme of sensuous adventure. By deficient eyes she is reduced to inferior states; by the evil eye of ignorance she is spell-bound to banality and ugliness. But she is redeemed by the eyes of understanding. The hero can take her as she is, without undue commotion, but with the kindness and assurance she requires, is potentially the King, the incarnate god, of her created world." *Hero*, 116 "[T]he whole sense of the ubiquitous myth of the hero's passage is that

it shall serve as a general pattern for men and women, wherever they may stand along the scale." *Hero*, 121.

73. How far this rationalizing element dictates to the modern theory of myth may be gathered from the extreme views of Levi-Strauss who, in insisting on "the unique cognitive status of myth", went so far as to see myth as possessed of "its own entelechy" and so "explained by nothing except "myth"". Thus myth is, in the end, its own "meta-language…as fully rational as any other communication", though, according to Levi-Strauss, it took the "super-rationalism" of Freud to allow us to see the possibility of reaching such "knowledge". See Stenski, *Four Theories*, 152-158. This insistent rationalizing of mythical consciousness has carried over also into the literary criticism on Graves, especially in more recent years, even among those who otherwise profess an intense admiration of his work. Thus we have watched Graves's life-long poetic effort to express himself in his relationship to the Goddess reduced to a matter of the deliberate cultivation of "ineffability"; his effort to present the Goddess in his book, *The White Goddess*, to a need to create "fixity", while his apparent renunciation of "the high mythopoeic mode" in his late poetry has been seen as a deliberate "effacement" and "erasure" intended to overcome a sort of Sisyphean repetition to which Graves must have felt condemned in continually re-stating the "one story":

> "the force of the accumulation of similes, metaphors, traces, marks, black and white of Graves's writings, is that it obliges readers to interpret the ineffability of the Triple Muse as a meaningful function within a larger semiotic system."

> "Graves was certainly perceptive enough to know that the link between words and things can never be fixed, that poetry and truth make two—yet he chose to fix it, and to write within that fixity. *The White Goddess* is a monument to that fixity…"

> "the advent of the Black Goddess is marked in the verse by a deliberate effacement of the language of the high mythopoeic mode in favor of a discourse which strips away many of the outward trappings

of myth...[It] spells possible release from the lifelong obligation to write a muse-poetry *which is condemned to do little more than generate restatements* of the recurring monomyth. The Black Goddess exists, therefore, as in one sense the end of myth, the simultaneous completion and erasure of the single poetic theme,..." [Italics mine.]

In the case of the first and third quotations, see Robert A. Davis "The Black Goddess" from *Graves and the Goddess*, ed., Ian Firla and Grevel Lindop, Selinsgrove, Susquehanna Univ. Press, 2003, 109-111. In the case of the second quotation, Andrew Painter, "How and Why Graves Proceeded in Poetry", also from *Graves and the Goddess*, 149.

For my critique of the easy view of late Graves as voiced by Davis here, see my *Debacle*, 71-75.

74. *Goddess*, 476.
75. *Goddess*, 455.
76. *Goddess*, 6.
77. See, for example, "This Holy Month". The need to counterbalance the energy with some form of right consciousness is implied in Graves's qualification above concerning the Western disposition to rationalism: cf. "not *altogether* happy."
78. See Nick Gammage "The Nature of the Goddess: Ted Hughes and Robert Graves" from *New Perspectives on Robert Graves*, ed. Patrick J. Quinn, Selinsgrove: Susquehanna Univ. Press, 1999, 151.
79. Gammage, 151.
80. Gammage (151) quotes Hughes from his "Interview with Ekbert Fass" from *The London Magazine*, January, 1971: "If you accept the energy, it destroys you. What is the alternative? To accept the energy and find methods of turning it to good, or keeping it under control—rituals, the machinery of religion. The old method is the only one."
81. See, along with "The End of Play", "No More Ghosts" and "To the Sovereign Muse".
82. "To the Sovereign Muse":
This was to praise you, Sovereign muse,
And to your love our pride devote,
83. How much alone see *The Modern Debacle*.

84. *Goddess*, 496.
85. *Goddess*, 499.
86. *Goddess*, 398.
87. *Goddess*, 399.
88. According to Hughes we need to see our way beyond the conflict (for the moment theoretically) by embracing Shakespeare's projection of how it finally resolves: "Since this great Court case is, as it were, still unfinished, the reader (like Shakespeare, and like my book, I trust) will have to make efforts to surmount the quarrel, and embrace Shakespeare's final judgement." *Shakespeare and the Goddess of Complete Being*, London: Faber, 1992, 44.
89. *Shakespeare and the Goddess*, 15.
90. *Shakespeare and the Goddess*, 15.
91. *Shakespeare and the Goddess*, 50.
92. See also Gammage (156-157): "Hughes…describes how… rejection of the diabolic—part of the Goddess of total unconditional love—is actually the rejection of [the hero's] own soul…The hero, Hughes argues, cannot separate the two aspects of the goddess—the creative and the destructive—and so ends up rejecting both…"
93. Suggesting that there was no other way to see it for what it is than to live through the consequences of it.
94. *Shakespeare and the Goddess*, 43.
95. With this shift in my argument, following Shakespeare's lead, I now embark on a more radical view of our *general* implication in guilt, man's *and* woman's, even if the human tragedy, as Shakespeare saw this, is brought to our view by man. It is also clear, as we shall see, that for Shakespeare only woman can finally bring us out of this human tragedy as we have inherited it.
96. It is typical of Graves's already advanced view of this situation that he does not even credit Macbeth with murdering Duncan. In his view it is Lady Macbeth who commits the murder under the influence of an avenging Goddess who is showing Herself again against the pretentious dominance of rational man and very naturally disposing of him: "for it is her spirit that takes possession of Lady Macbeth and inspires her to murder King Duncan". *The White Goddess*, 417. Hughes has it literally the same way but is himself anxious to bring out the whole process by which man has gotten himself into that condition. He speaks "of Lady Macbeth as Queen of Hell. Possessed by the powers of the Goddess (who was

rejected before the play began), her avenging fury has already marked down the rational 'ruler' of the Adonis world that rejected her...[N]ot only will Macbeth's Adonis persona have to die, but Duncan and Banquo too." *Shakespeare and the Goddess*, 246.
97. *Shakespeare and the Goddess*, 84.
98. See *If It Were Done: 'Macbeth' and Tragic Action*, Amherst: University of Massachusetts Press, 1986, 81.
"Sacred to the gods", and, one must add, to the Goddess: her association with war is a staple of the lore about her. See Balas, 169*passim*.
99. *If It Were Done*, 82.
100. *If It Were Done* 79, 77.
101. *If It Were Done* 84. Clearly a point on which Calderwood distinguishes himself from another great theorist of sacrificial ritual, Rene Girard, whose focus is precisely on the ritual value of "scapegoat victims". See his *Violence and the Sacred*, Baltimore: Johns Hopkins University Press, 1977.
102. *If It Were Done*, 89.
103. See "The Early Scenes of 'Macbeth': Preface to a New Interpretation", *English Literary History*, 47, 1980, 26: "Among the benefits that flow from the king to his subjects are bloody occasions. His vassals are under obligation to him for the chance to fight and kill, to die nobly, to show valor and loyalty, to contend with others in manliness, to compete for reputation and honors by which valor is rewarded...Bloodshed is the proof of manliness and the source of honor and reputation. Bloodshed, bloodiness, bloody-mindedness quicken the pulse of the social order and sharpen its edge."
104. Thus Berger says of the role of the king in *Macbeth*: "The more his subjects do for him, the more he must do for them; the more he does for them, feeding their ambition and their power, the less secure can he be of his mastery." (24-25) "All seem aware of the precariousness of the symbiotic relation to the king..." (28)
105. See Johannes Huizinga, *The Waning of the Middle Ages*, London: Edward Arnold, 1955 (orig.pub., 1924) 18: "Pride...the sin of the feudal and hierarchic age..." See also *Homo Ludens*, Boston: Beacon Press, 1955, 111-112 : " pride and vainglory, the desire for prestige and all the pomp of superiority."
106. *The Waning of the Middle Ages*, 96. Cf. Jung, *Symbols*: "symbol-formation...has no meaning whatever unless it strives against the

resistance of instinct, just as undisciplined instincts would bring nothing but ruin to man if the symbol did not give them form." (228); "the old brutality returns in force..." (230)
107. *The Waning of the Middle Ages*, 40.
108. "That reality has constantly given the lie to these high illusions of a pure and noble social life, who would deny? But where should we be, if our thoughts had never transcended the exact limits of the feasible?" *The Waning of the Middle Ages*, 94. "For the history of civilization the perennial dream of a sublime life has the value of a very important reality." (82)
109. Cf. I.iv: "There if I grow, / The harvest is your own." It is significant in this respect that both in Holinshed/Boece and in Buchanan, the immediate sources on which Shakespeare drew for *Macbeth*, the murder of Duncan *involves* Banquo as an accomplice. Shakespeare clearly had his own emphasis to make.
110. *If It Were Done*, 84.
111. Thus, to adapt a phrase from Bradley, "the despair of a man who [has] knowingly made war on his own soul": A.C. Bradley, *Shakespearean Tragedy*, New York: St. Martin's Press, 1978, orig. pub. 1904, 359.
112. See J.I.M. Stewart, *Character and Motive in Shakespeare*, Longmans, 1949, 93: "The thought of murdering Duncan, first or new glimpsed in the recesses of his mind at the prompting of the witches, produces violent somatic disturbance, as the prospect of a ritual act of cannibalism may do in a Kwakiutl Indian."
113. As in the banquet scene where the Ghost of Banquo appears to him. Cf., also, III.ii: "these terrible dreams/That shake us nightly."
114. Cf. III.iv.
115. See *Shakespeare*, London: Jonathan Cape, 1959, orig. pub. 1936, 325. The scene in question is II.ii, when Macbeth enters having just murdered Duncan.
116. For a fuller exposition of this dominant process in Shakespeare, see my *Othello's Sacrifice* (Toronto: Guernica, 1996), Part Three, 77*passim*.
117. I elaborate further on this viewpoint in *Shakespeare, the Goddess, and Modernity*, which is to appear under the IUniverse imprint concurrently with this second edition of *Impasse*: see the chapter "On King Lear".
118. Ferocity, a sensual quality, is a definite aspect of Cordelia's character which she shares with the whole of the Lear-family,

qualified though the ferocity is in her case by a more deep-set goodness. Cf. V.iii: "Shall we not see these daughters and these sisters?"

119. See my *Shakespeare's Muse*, New York: IUniverse, 2007, 22-23.
120. See *Shakespeare's Muse*, 8-9, also my "Preface on *Hamlet* and Luther" in *Otherworldly Hamlet*, Montreal: Guernica, 1991, 15ff.
121. Another kind of love, of the spirit, will have to emerge from human nature. This is the ultimate end of the tragic process in Shakespeare, as I show in Part Three of *Othello's Sacrifice*, 87*passim*.
122. See my chapter on "Sexuality" in *Otherworldly Hamlet*, 50ff.
123. More on this in *Shakespeare's Muse*, 22ff, and in my monograph, *On Luther*, Ottawa: Heart's Core Publications, 2009 (see the section on *Othello*), 44ff.
124. For an elaborate discussion of Shakespeare's complex relation to Luther see *Shakespeare's Muse*, 8-11;27-28. See also *Othello's Sacrifice*, 80-81.
    Clearly, Shakespeare goes on to deal with the fall into human nature in his own highly characteristic way, being his own tragic visionary.
125. One needs to see for oneself how Hughes perceives Shakespeare's experience taking shape with every play that came from his hand from *Hamlet* onwards.
126. How the conflict of feelings between Graves and his beloved is handled in "Eurydice" is a case in point. In this poem Graves appears to be almost reached by the influence of passion as experienced by the Shakespearean (and the general Elizabethan) hero. At some point the poet expresses himself in the same bitter contempt and hatred of the beloved, for her betrayal of their shared ideals:
    > *Look where she shines with a borrowed blaze of light*
    > *Among the cowardly, faceless, lost, unright*
    > ....
    > *She has gnawn at corpse-flesh till her breath stank,*
    > *Paired with a jackal, grown distraught and lank*

    The beloved has *wandered* from them, disloyal to their cause, and the poet has come to the limits of his endurance in watching their love betrayed. Even so, Graves cannot let himself be taken away with his feelings, abiding in the simplicity of his unshakeable allegiance to his Goddess, whom he will not allow to be forsworn—no matter what the cost, even should this be, metaphorically-speaking, his own head (as Orpheus lost his to the frenzied Bachannals who here represent the beloved's own power to destroy him by persisting in her betrayal; in that case he will be left then to his singing, for *later* generations to understand):

My own dear heart, dare you so war on me
As to strangle love in a mad perversity?
Is ours a fate can ever be forsworn
Though my lopped head sing to the yet unborn?

Graves is so persuaded that it is man who, even in such circumstances, fails to understand the beloved, is so given up to the idea that man must refuse his own demands on the Goddess, that he must see to it that himself is strangled in his own passion of revolt, as another poem, "Myrrhina" clarifies:

O, why judge Myrrhina
As though she were a man?
She obeys a dark wisdom
(As Eve did before her)
Which never can fail,
Being bound by no pride
Of armorial bearings
Bequeathed in tail male.
And though your blood brother
Who dared to do you wrong
In his greed of Myrrhina
Might plead a like wisdom
The fault to excuse,
Myrrhina is just:
She has hanged the poor rogue
By the neck from her noose.

But there is much ambiguity in "Eurydice". The poet speaks of a 'scene' of violent passion between himself and the beloved:

In a mirror I watch blood trickling down the wall—

confronted by which, the poet asks:

Is it mine?

This might read, and was probably intended to be read, as suggesting that the poet remains superciliously unaffected by the beloved's violence and beyond its power to destroy his faith, as the rest of the line seems to clarify:

Yet still I stand here, proud and tall.

The destructive import of this passion is thus simply put away by Graves, as an affront to the incontrovertible will of the Goddess (to which the beloved's passion is thus referred).

But has Graves not in this but denied a passion that might otherwise as validly have claimed his attention as evidence of a hopeless reality—which, we may suppose, has not gone away only because it has been thought away? Might the poem not even be thought to suggest that the poet himself has indulged in vengeful passion? I must confess that initially I read the poem as confessing as much, though the poet does turn away from the passion in the end, one way or the other. For why ask "Is it mine?", as if to suggest that perhaps it may not be, being in that case her blood, which *he* has spilled? The poet might simply have said: "It is mine." There would have been no ambiguity then. Can we see in this ambiguous effect, in fact, some form of implied confession of violence in himself?

127. Gammage, 151.
128. Many of the earlier plays are echoed in passages from the last plays: e.g., *Macbeth* in the scene between Cleon and Dionyza in *Pericles*; *King Lear* in the scene of recognition between Pericles and Marina; *Othello*, of course, in *The Winter's Tale*; *Hamlet* and *Macbeth* in *The Tempest*.
129. See *Othello's Sacrifice*, 88ff. for a full treatment of this whole evolution, which I can only outline here.
130. In Her medieval and Renaissance manifestations, the Goddess appears typically in the form of a Virgin, reflecting the purifying process with which She is by then also connected, apart from the more material (sometimes perversely material) forms She takes in Graves's history. Diana, especially as Diana of Ephesus, is in this respect a classical prototype of Her later form. Such developments substantiate that additional evolution of the Goddess *into* the Sophia as Erich Neumann once pictured this:

> *The dual Great Goddess as mother and daughter can so far transform her original bond with the elementary character as to become a pure feminine spirit, a kind of Sophia, a spiritual whole in which all heaviness and materiality are transcended. Then she not only forms the earth and heaven of the retort that we call life, and is not only the whirling wheel revolving within it, but is also the supreme essence and distillation to which life in this world can be transformed.*

All this is, what's more, also relative to what mankind can make of itself:

> *The Archetypal Feminine in man unfolds like mankind itself. At the beginning stands the primeval goddess, resting in the materiality of her elementary character… at the end is Tara[-Sophia]…an eternal image of the redeeming female spirit. Both together form the unity of the Great Goddess who, in the totality of her unfolding, fills the world from its lowest elementary phase to its supreme spiritual transformation.*
>
> *The Great Mother*, Princeton: Princeton Univ. Press, 1955, 334-335.

Goddess lore as a whole will confirm that chastity alone is the quality that ever allowed direct access to the Goddess. See Balas, 177*passim*.

131. See *Othello's Sacrifice*, 97ff for more on this.
132. See *Othello's Sacrifice*, 96, for an elaboration on this.
133. Even Antonio, the worst of the conspirators, is drawn into this impression. However, I do not pretend to claim that Shakespeare feels that literally all can be set right again. It is clear that in the end Antonio and perhaps also Sebastian (Stephano, and Trinculo) do *not* come along: there is an aspect of the human will that finally resists reformation. However, this Shakespeare recognizes as the ultimate human problem only the more clearly now that his has become the will to ultimate harmony.
134. The conflict between the ideal and the earthly, as well as their potential mutual impenetrability one by the other, all in connection with an attainable Goddess who engages the poet on these issues, is a staple of the Romantic Imagination generally. In this respect Endymion's quest for his Goddess may be fruitfully compared, e.g., with Heinrich's quest in Novalis's *Heinrich von Ofterdingen*, or that of the hero in Shelley's *Epipsychidion*. Behind this extensive presentation in Romantic literature lies the story of the Goddess as summarized, e.g., by Cartari in his *Images of the Gods of the Ancients* (see Balas, 190):

> *The story goes…that the goddess possessed a pure and chaste love for [a] young man [Attis], and gave this to him along with the charge of caring for all her sacred things, on the condition that he preserve his virginity and modesty for all time. And this he promised to*

> do and swore to uphold the obligation. But the poor wretch did not observe his vow, but instead fell in love with a beautiful nymph, daughter of the river Sangarius in that country. He remembered the promise made to the goddess, but nevertheless took pleasure in his new love.

135. See Walter Jackson Bate, *John Keats*, Cambridge, Massachusetts: Harvard University Press, 1964, 390.
136. See *The White Goddess*, 418ff.
137. *John Keats*, 333.
138. *John Keats*, 374.
139. *John Keats*, 391.
140. *John Keats*, 322.
141. *John Keats*, 324.
142. *John Keats*, 322.
143. *John Keats*, 494.
144. *John Keats*, 322.
145. In this aspect, at least, Keats had convincingly filled in the evolutionary story on which he was epically bent originally.
146. "To this point Wordsworth had come…when he wrote "Tintern Abbey" and it seems to me his genius is explorative of those dark Passages." (Letter of 3 May, 1818.)
147. Keats's approach is in this the *opposite* of Shakespeare's for whom the illuminating consciousness is provided from without, from a point that is always, at any given moment, finally outside his own immediate inner life, as we have seen above, 49.
148. It is very possible that Keats invented this "Grecian" urn.
149. Coleridge reflects a similar experience to us in his "Christabel", which must have served as one source of inspiration for Keats when writing his poem.
150. Unable to marry for lack of a proper profession at this time, Keats had conceived of "Lamia" as a way of establishing himself with a wider reading public and so achieving some financial independence.
151. For the influence of Keats's ideas in this poem on later 19th century aesthetics, see Frank Kermode, *Romantic Image*, London: Routledge, 1957.
152. One thinks, pre-eminently, of Shelley's *Prometheus Unbound*.
153. Keats was generally under Coleridge's influence at this time. See Beth Lau, *Keats's Reading of the Romantic Poets*, Ann Arbor: University of Michigan Press, 1991, 85-86. See, also, Jack

Stillinger, "Keats and Coleridge" from *Coleridge, Keats and the Imagination*, ed., J. Robert Barth, S.J., and John L. Mahoney, Columbia: University of Missouri Press, 1990.
154. In "The Excursion".
155. *Keats*, London: Jonathan Cape, 1955, 279.
156. *Keats*, 283.
157. See. e.g., Glen O. Allen, "The Fall of Endymion: A Study in Keats's Intellectual Growth" from the *Keats-Shelley Journal*, Vol. VI, Winter, 1957, 57: "Keats exchanged his ethereal attachments for his earthly ones..." Or Jack Stillinger, "Keats and Coleridge", 27: "his scepticism toward the visionary in practically all his major narrative and lyrics of 1819 is tantamount to an acceptance of the naturalized imagination central in the poetry and theories of Coleridge and Wordsworth rather than with the more transcendental and visionary schemes of Blake and Shelley." Yet cf. Allen Tate, "On the Limits of Poetry" from *Collected Literary Essays*, Denver: Colorado, 1959, 163-164, who only wished Keats had been more capable in this direction: "His goddess, insofar as she is more than a decorative symbol in Keats, was all Uranian... His pictorial and sculpturesque effects, which arrest time into space, tend to remove from experience the dramatic agitation of Aphrodite Pandemos, whose favors are granted and whose woes are counted in the actuality of time." "In Keats's mind... there was, to put it in the simplest language, a strong compulsion towards the realization of physical love, but he could not reconcile it with his idealization of the beloved." 163-164.
158. Both of whom were much taken with "Hyperion" (i.e., its first version, the only one to be published in Keats's lifetime). Byron compared some of its passages to Aeschylus.
159. Back to pre-Minoan times, in comparison with Keats who was drawing on Classical lore.
160. See Graves, *Poetic Craft and Principle*, London: Cassell, 1967, 135.
161. See Kermode, *Romantic Image*, 8; "Moneta, I take it, represents the survival of the archaic way of thought—imaginative rather than discursive ("the large utterance of the early gods"), *un-dissociated*, mythopoeic; more profound, though certainly, to use the word in a limiting sense, less *human* than the discourse of 'philosophy' which Keats, with his tentative evolutionism, was trying to accept as a necessary human development."